# HOW TO DEAL WITH
# DISCIPLINE
# PROBLEMS

## IN THE SCHOOLS

## A Practical Guide
## for Educators

By Michael R. Valentine, Ph.D.

KENDALL/HUNT PUBLISHING COMPANY
2460 Kerper Boulevard P.O. Box 539 Dubuque, Iowa 52004-0539

LB 3011
.V28
1987

This edition has been printed directly from camera-ready copy.

Copyright © 1987 by Michael R. Valentine

Library of Congress Catalog Card Number: 89–84210

ISBN 0–8403–5340–5

Printed in the United States of America
10   9   8   7   6   5   4   3   2

Dedicated to my parents,
George and Helen Valentine.

# TABLE OF CONTENTS

# ACKNOWLEDGEMENTS

I would like to acknowledge my indebtedness and appreciation to the many people whose assistance made this book possible. First, I would like to thank Dr. Paul Wood, who changed the direction of my professional career by introducing me to this most powerful and interesting family-systems counseling model. Second, I would like to thank Nancy Hubbell, Genine Keene, and Sue Belles for their time and energy in editing the manuscript. I am indebted and particularly grateful to Sue Leahy, Dr. Tom Kampwirth, and Nancy Hubbell for their many ideas and suggestions to improve the book. Further, I am grateful to my wife, Gail, and to my secretary, Marie Hill, who provided expert typing skills and patience throughout the many drafts of the manuscript. Third, I would like to acknowledge my appreciation to the many teachers, principals, students, and parents who have shared their stories and their experiences.

My special gratitude goes to Vic Braden and his staff at the Vic Braden Tennis College, who (unknown to themselves) have saved my mental health many times by letting me work for them part-time as a tennis instructor.

Special thanks go to Dr. Ken Weisbrod, retired Dean of Counseling and Testing at California State University at Long Beach, and to Dr. James Trent, Professor of Education at the University of California at Los Angeles. Both of these educators have had such a profound influence on my personal and professional growth and development that I feel a part of this book was completed for them in honor and recognition of the faith, belief, and trust which they had in me that flamed my desire to become something more than I was.

And—last in order, but surely first in my heart—I give a special thanks to my family: to my parents for the love, support, and encouragement that they gave to me throughout my life; to my wife, Gail, who patiently and understandingly supported and encouraged the completion of this goal over the past five years; and, finally, to Scott and Todd, who often had to wait many hours before Daddy could come out and play.

# PREFACE

Everyone in education knows that solving discipline problems is consistently rated as a top priority facing the schools of this country. Both critics and supporters of public education agree that good discipline is an essential condition if the business of the schools is to go forward efficiently and productively.

The effects of classroom discipline problems have taken their toll on teacher morale with resultant stress, burn-out, absenteeism, early retirement, and change of profession. Besides affecting teachers, these discipline-related problems have had direct and indirect effects on students' academic performance, behavior, and sense of well-being and ultimate human potential.

This book is designed to address in a concrete, specific, practical way the problems which teachers face every day. It is not a theoretical dissertation nor an ivory-tower abstract speculation. It contains no new psychological jargon or intervention techniques that require months or years of studying and perfecting before one can implement them in the classroom.

This method is, on the other hand, a practical, common-sense approach based on the power of clear, straightforward, direct communication and back-up techniques. It is designed to be used by real people in actual settings in real classrooms.

Here is a method which does not rely on psychodynamic understanding, behavior-modification techniques, or paraphernalia such as stars, candy, prizes, or marbles in a jar to stop students' inappropriate behavior. Instead, it focuses on actual teacher/ student communication and interaction patterns. It looks at what teachers actually say and do when a student is acting inappropriately, and it compares and contrasts effective and ineffective patterns of communication and interaction.

The purpose of this book is to give teachers and other school personnel the ability to stop students' inappropriate behavior, thereby enabling teachers to regain and/or to maintain control of their classrooms and to improve student performance in both the academic and behavioral areas. This book does *not* present a comprehensive classroom-management approach. It does not deal with instructional, curricular, or methodological matters. It does not treat environmental factors and/or teacher or student personality styles or characteristics. Even though these factors are important in their own right and help to maintain classroom control, the present approach assumes that they are not the most important variables in initially stopping inappropriate behavior.

There are schools which have good curricula, great reading programs, and well-qualified teachers, but nevertheless because of extreme discipline problems are unable to utilize these positive resources effectively. If students are "out of control", refuse to pay attention, or will not study, then very little learning will take place. This book assumes that stopping students' inappropriate behavior is the foundation of an effective educational institution. It further assumes that if students are well behaved, on task, and behaving appropriately in the classroom, then they will learn more with or without the latest educational techniques, methodologies, or fads. Therefore, the major focus of this book will be on how to stop inappropriate behavior, to get students on task, to keep them on task, and to get teachers to gain control of the classroom and of the school.

This book will provide the *foundation* for a more effective education. It will then be up to the teachers and the district administrators, along with such other key resources as books and instructional programs, to provide the superstructure of more effective education in order to maximize student potential.

Chapter I provides an overview of the program, together with presenting the major assumptions of this approach.

In Chapter II the first major component of this approach—analysis of common belief-systems about the reasons why children misbehave—will be explored in considerable detail. This procedure will show that certain common belief-systems are not substantiated by observable evidence. In fact, these erroneous belief-systems first imply that the child is incapable of controlling himself and then become an excuse for allowing the student to misbehave.

Chapter III analyzes actual teacher/student interactions and communication patterns that are either effective or ineffective in stopping inappropriate behavior. This chapter demonstrates that when the teacher—because of an erroneous belief-system—believes a student to be incapable, she uses vague, abstract, and indirect communications patterns rather than clear, concrete, and direct messages.

Chapter IV explores effective communication patterns that stop inappropriate behavior and contrasts these with the ineffective communications patterns which were presented in Chapter III.

Chapter V explores how to incorporate the information learned up to this point into actual classroom-management techniques. It also explores effective back-up techniques that teachers can use when a clear, direct message does not seem to work. It shows teachers how to develop an individual discipline lesson-plan which involves other school personnel or parents in stopping the student's inappropriate behavior. It shows teachers how they can develop and use effective back-up techniques which focus on solving the real problem rather than relying on traditional school intervention techniques that punish the student.

Chapter VI provides specific suggestions and case-study examples of solutions and back-up techniques to school-related academic and behavioral problems, including truancy, fights, and poor academic performance.

Finally, Chapter VII answers specific questions and concerns which teachers have brought up in connection with this model.

One last general comment concludes this Preface:As a way to keep a consistent perspective and viewpoint, and to reduce confusion over pronouns, I decided to refer to the teacher or other adult as "she" and to refer to the student or other child as "he". This simplification has been done in order to keep clear (in the minds of both reader and writer!) the interactions between adult and child without having constantly to change sexes and/or perspectives.

# CHAPTER I:  Introduction

"If you don't do these ten problems in the next ten minutes, you're staying after school to finish them."

"Try to get to class on time."

"If you respected me, you wouldn't do that."

"How many times am I going to have to tell you before you start to grow up and act your age?"

"You do that one more time and I'm sending you to the principal."

"I bet you'll think twice before you do something stupid like that again."

"You are older than the rest of the students. You should know better. I'm really disappointed in you. After all I've done for you, I can't believe you would do this to me."

"I want you to get to class on time and do your work."

"Why are you fighting?"

"I can see you are out of your seat again for the hundredth time."

These and thousands of other vague and indirect communications are used daily by school personnel, parents, and other adults in the hope that such statements will influence the student in some positive way and thereby get him to stop his inappropriate behavior.

It is the contention of this book that adult/student interactions and communications such as these do not work well at stopping inappropriate behavior, especially for those students who have had long histories of school difficulties. When communications such as the above are systematically analyzed, it becomes obvious that the messages given are vague, abstract, and indirect rather than clear directives to stop the inappropriate behavior. It is a further contention that students who are having difficulty in school need structure, guidance, and very *clear, direct, specific, concrete* communications to insure that they get back on track to being successful at school.

This particular discipline approach is based on analysis of direct interaction and communication patterns rather than on behavior modification or any psychodynamically oriented approach. It is an easily learned, straightforward, simple, yet very powerful method of stopping most inappropriate student behavior immediately. It can be used by teachers in the classroom, parents at home, and administrators, guidance counselors, psychologists, and others who consult with parents and teachers. This approach teaches how to analyze actual communication patterns that are either effective or ineffective in stopping inappropriate behavior. It also teaches the reader how to avoid manipulations by the student, how to use simple but very effective school-based intervention and back-up techniques to stop most inappropriate behavior, and how to run a highly structured parent/teacher/student conference designed to elicit parental support to stop the student's inappropriate behavior when the school-based interventions do not seem to work.

One of the basic tenets of this communications-based approach states that the actual words which are used to try to stop inappropriate behavior reflect an underlying conceptual framework, value-system, or belief-system. The speaker's belief then predisposes him/her to perceive reality in a certain way and to expect certain behaviors.

Beliefs and concepts about the world are linked intrinsically to our choice of words, interactions, and communication patterns. For the most part, we act and communicate congruently with what we believe. Therefore, if we wish to change the way in which we act and communicate to students, we must examine and question our beliefs about the causes of the student's inappropriate behavior. It is the contention of this book that if most of the popularly held beliefs of why students misbehave were to be objectively examined, then little or no evidence would be found to support the beliefs. Success at objectively evaluating, challenging, and eroding these popular beliefs would then leave open the possibility of communicating and acting in a totally different manner. Such changes in beliefs and communication patterns would then set the stage to stop most of the student's inappropriate behavior quickly.

The logic of this system is simple: If you believe that the student is incapable of doing what you want him to do, then you will not directly and clearly tell him to do what you want him to do. For example, if you believe that a student is hyperactive and unable to sit still, then you will not tell him to sit still. Such an order would be incongruent with your belief that he is hyperactive and unable to sit still. However, if the belief-system is challenged by objectively collecting evidence and thereby proving that the student is in control of his behavior and is capable of sitting still, then it becomes reasonable and congruent with the new way of seeing things to tell the student in very specific and concrete terms to sit still. This new way of seeing the student as being capable then enables the direct communications patterns or statements to be backed up, if need be, with actions that convey to the student that he is to do as he is told.

This basic tenet—that words used to correct inappropriate behavior are a reflection of an underlying value-system, belief-system, or world-view—forms the foundation of the different intervention strategies of this approach. The following chapters explore this basic tenet in greater depth and illustrate how it can be applied to school-related discipline problems in very practical and concrete ways.

Table I presents a flow chart that gives an overview of the total school-based intervention plan. The flow chart is divided into four Levels. In Level One, a general philosophical orientation of the principles of the approach is given to three different target populations: parents, school personnel, and appropriate community resources.

In Level Two, more specific classroom and school-based skills, interventions, and back-up techniques are given to teachers and school personnel to increase the chances of successfully getting the students back on track behaviorally and academically.

Level Three of this model deals with the relatively small percentage of students who are unresponsive to school-based teacher interventions. Here a referral is made to the counselor and/or the school psychologist so that she can run a highly structured brief family counseling session designed to have the parents see that—if they wish to do so—they can get their child to act appropriately and to do what they want him to do.

If the counseling sessions do not seem to work and the parents are unable or unwilling to get the child under control, then Level Four of the model is implemented (administrative and community interventions).

The flow chart and the intervention program follow a few simple principles. If your intervention works, it works. If it does not work, keep trying something else until something does work. Never use more control or force than is necessary. Start with the simple and obvious explanations and interventions. If these do not work, move to the more complex, sophisticated, and subtle interventions. The intervention structure of this approach is like a path analysis which branches into two possible outcomes. One, the intervention works, and the student is back on task being successful; or two, the intervention does not work, and the student is still acting inappropriately. If the intervention does not work at one particular level, the philosophy is to continue to use interventions within that level but to add the structure and interventions of the next level until you get the student back on task.

This book will focus primarily on Level One, the general underlying principles of the approach, and on Level Two, teacher and school-based intervention skills and strategies.

A brief orientation to Levels Three and Four will be presented so that the reader will have an overview of the total program, but a more in-depth explanation of Levels Three and Four is presented in the book *How to Deal*

## School-based Intervention Plan

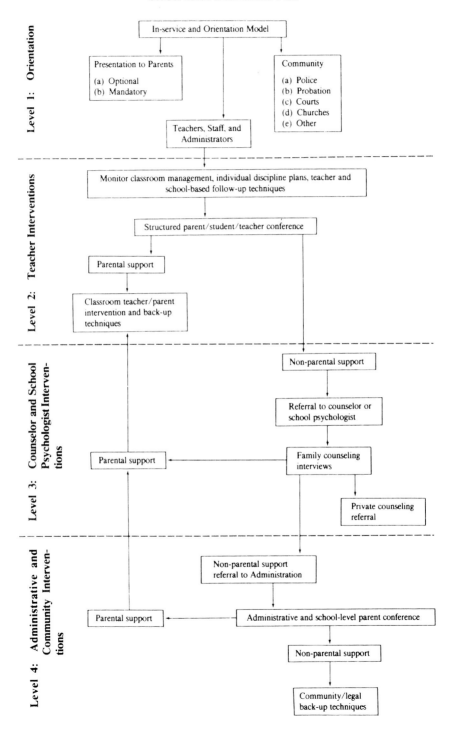

Level 1: Orientation

In-service and Orientation Model

Presentation to Parents
(a) Optional
(b) Mandatory

Community
(a) Police
(b) Probation
(c) Courts
(d) Churches
(e) Other

Teachers, Staff, and Administrators

Level 2: Teacher Interventions

Monitor classroom management, individual discipline plans, teacher and school-based follow-up techniques

Structured parent/student/teacher conference

Parental support

Classroom teacher/parent intervention and back-up techniques

Level 3: Counselor and School Psychologist Interventions

Non-parental support

Referral to counselor or school psychologist

Parental support

Family counseling interviews

Private counseling referral

Level 4: Administrative and Community Interventions

Non-parental support referral to Administration

Parental support

Administrative and school-level parent conference

Non-parental support

Community/legal back-up techniques

*with Difficult Discipline Problems: A Family-Systems Approach,* which is designed specifically for school counselors, psychologists, and administrators.

The first step in developing effective interventions, regardless of which level of the model you are operating from, is to have a firm understanding of how beliefs and communication patterns are intrinsically linked. In the next three chapters, methods of analyzing beliefs and communication patterns will be presented. Understanding how to analyze erroneous beliefs and ineffective communication patterns will then give parents, teachers, school psychologists, and administrators the foundation for implementing effective back-up techniques and strategies to help to solve a wide range of school-related problems.

# Chapter II:  Erroneous Belief-Systems

In order to change patterns of communication with students, the teacher or any other responsible adult first must analyze her erroneous and inappropriate belief-systems about the reasons why students misbehave. The intent of this procedure is to challenge those belief-systems and to erode them so that they can no longer be used as excuses for allowing the student to act inappropriately. When the teacher changes her beliefs about why students misbehave, she becomes open to the possibility of perceiving the student in a different light, thereby setting the stage for change in both her behavior and the student's behavior.

Before the teacher can effectively analyze her beliefs about why students misbehave, she needs to understand how trait-attribute theory and the labeling process work. This process can be understood readily if one looks at the drawing below and notices how perceptions change as labels change.

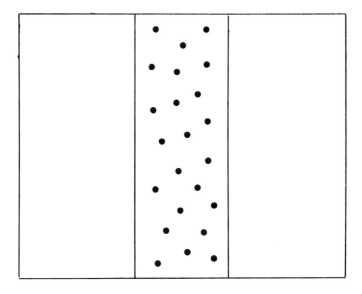

What does the drawing represent? Look at it awhile before proceeding.

Is it a picture of flies stuck to fly-paper?

A giraffe neck passing a second-story window?

A window with curtains half open, revealing snowflakes falling outside?

Germs under a microscope?

People seen from the top of a twenty-story building?

A partially open observatory dome, showing the stars?

Although the lines and dots of the figure never change, one begins to perceive them differently once a word, a label, a trait, a concept, or a belief is attached. In response to the suggestion that the drawing is a giraffe neck passing a second-story window, one sees it as a giraffe. In a real situation, one would act as if it were a giraffe. One begins to see it, to believe it, and to react and feel toward it as if it were a giraffe.

If the words, concepts, and beliefs are changed because someone reports that it is a window with the curtains half open, revealing falling snow, then the picture is perceived as something completely different from a giraffe.

The drawing has never changed as we considered it, but conceptions of it change drastically with the new words, ideas, or beliefs. Adults' conceptions and labeling of children's behavior follow a similar pattern. Children are children. They play doctor, and some parents label them sexual perverts. Often adults project their own fears and anxieties about sexuality onto children and label them—and then tend to see them as if the children were the label. A child steals one time, and his father says, "The kid is going to be a thief." The problem is no longer just the behavior but the fact that adults label the child who exhibits the behavior, see him as if the label were true, and then act accordingly. Suddenly, the child is perverted, he is clumsy, he is a thief, he is stupid. Adults give him a label, and that label provides a way of seeing and understanding his behavior. Once an adult adopts a certain perspective, she is locked into seeing the child in a way that has profound consequences.

Once an adult has established a belief-system, she will act and interact congruently with that belief-system. When she begins to interact with the child based on a particular belief-system, then she has an image of that child—either positive or negative—that corresponds to her belief. As a result, the child begins to conform to the image. In order to change the belief-system (and subsequently her interactions with the child), the adult must challenge the negative, inappropriate belief-system, her image of the child, and the truth of her belief. She must investigate carefully to establish whether or not substantial evidence to support the belief actually exists.

Everyone has been programed by significant others, either positively or negatively, to believe certain things about himself. Based on interactions within the family, the school, and the peer group, the child eventually internalizes the label and believes it himself. After days, months, years of labeling, he becomes that label to the people around him and to himself. Everyone has experienced this labeling to some extent. It is common to hear people say, "I'm not athletic", or "I'm very uncoordinated", "I'm not sexy", or "I'm not musical; I can't play a thing." People accept the programing and eventually program themselves and act accordingly. As a result of labeling, people give up on things which they might have done: they never touch a musical instrument or never play tennis again. However, if anyone played a musical instrument three hours a day, 365 days a year, then he would play that instrument much better than he had done the previous year whether he was "musical" or not. Many people, because of self-talk and labeling, put self-imposed limits on what they can and cannot do.

When people see themselves in a certain way and act accordingly, they don't spend the time and energy necessary to become better. Therefore, they must challenge their belief-systems in order to stop the cycle of limiting themselves and their students. In so doing they will increase their potential and that of their students. Remember that people speak and act congruently with the beliefs which they hold about the nature of things. Therefore, to change what they say and do about children's misbehavior, they have to change their inappropriate beliefs about why children misbehave.

Imagine that Mrs. Morgan believes that Jeff, a student in her fifth-grade classroom, has Parkinson's disease because she observed him shaking. Would she tell him to stop shaking? Probably she would not—because of her belief that he could not control his behavior. However, if Jeff always stopped shaking while talking to his best friend but shook during all other interactions, then what would Mrs. Morgan think? Probably she would question her belief that it was Parkinson's disease which caused Jeff to shake in all situations and that he thus had no control of his behavior.

This approach suggests that the teacher needs to look for the evidence to support her beliefs. If Jeff controls his shaking while talking to his best friend, she has visible proof that he has more control than she originally believed. The erroneous belief that he has Parkinson's disease contributes to maintaining the inappropriate behavior. When any responsible adult believes that a student is incapable of controlling his behavior, she acts congruently with that belief and therefore allows the behavior to continue. Conversely, when she believes that the student is capable of controlling his behavior, it then becomes reasonable for her to expect a change in behavior.

Finding that the evidence does not support her beliefs enables a teacher to change those beliefs. In so doing, she sees the student as being capable of change. The teacher's or other adult's change in orientation, as simple as it may seem, is crucial in changing the student's inappropriate behavior.

The following sections of this chapter will examine various belief-systems concerning why students misbehave and will challenge these beliefs by investigating and questioning the available evidence. The student and his behavior will remain the same; only the beliefs about the causes of his behavior will change.

Johnny, the student under examination, has severe behavior problems: he rolls around on the floor, has regular temper-tantrums, throws things, cusses at the teacher, sets fires, skips school, lies, cheats, steals, and of course makes poor grades.

Examining each erroneous belief-system as if it were the real reason and the only reason why Johnny is behaving as he is should help to clarify the implications which these various belief-systems have on teacher/student interaction patterns. Learning a structured way of analyzing belief-systems should help adults to discount erroneous beliefs so that it becomes reasonable for them to interact differently with the students and to expect, and if necessary to demand, appropriate changes in behavior.

In turn, we shall examine several belief-systems which are often cited to account for a student's misbehavior.

## Possession

In the first example, the real reason and the only reason for the student's bad behavior is that he is possessed by the Devil. Since most of us are not strongly involved in nor passionately committed to this particular belief, it can be dispassionately and logically dissected to see how it can affect our communication with and behavior toward the student. If the teacher adopts the belief that Johnny's behavior is the result of possession, one key question arises: Does she see the student as capable of controlling his own behavior? Yes or No? Answer: No. That answer is crucial because it predisposes her to act, think, and communicate in a certain way toward the student. When she doesn't see the student as being capable of controlling his own behavior, her interaction and communication patterns will be affected in predictable ways. Since she doesn't think that the student is capable of doing what she wants him to do, it is not reasonable for her to say, "Stop that and never do that again," or to take some other firm action to stop the behavior.

Following this line of logic, one goes on to ask the following questions: If Johnny is possessed, is the teacher going to be able to control or change his behavior? Is she the agent of change? If Johnny is not in control of his behavior, and the teacher is not in control of it or able to change it, what is she going to do with this student for the rest of the year? Think about it. The student is going to drive her absolutely crazy. What intervention strategies are available (behavior modification, time out, individual or group counseling, assertive discipline, isolation)? Probably the only reasonable strategy or intervention, given the teacher's belief-system, is some form of exorcism. (Or, as one teacher said, "She can beat the devil out of him.").

When the student has no control, the teacher has no control, and exorcism is the only reasonable intervention possible, is it reasonable for the teacher to be angry or to tell Johnny to stop the behavior and demand that he control himself? If she started getting angry at a student who was unable to control himself, she probably would feel bad about it. This teacher, like most adults, doesn't like to get angry or upset. Generally, she feels that it is wrong to do so. She tries to avoid confrontation, and wishes to be understanding, nice, kind, and pleasant. The student, however, continues the inappropriate behavior until she just can't take it any more, whereupon she explodes in anger. At this point she may make hostile comments which she will later regret.

The teacher comes away from her confrontation with Johnny with feelings of guilt and remorse. She mutters to herself, "Boy, I'm never going to do that again. I'm supposed to like and to help these kids. I came unglued; I need to get control of myself. I need a good shrink to help me to deal with my anger." Perhaps she actually will consult a psychologist to help her to deal with her anger, frustration, anxiety, stress, and burn-out.

It is appropriate, of course, to deal with frustrations and to try to become the best person possible besides. However, if the teacher gets the student under control and gets him to do as she asks, then she won't have to deal with so much anger and burn-out. It is unnecessary to spend time and money on psychoanalysis to figure out how to adjust to students who are behaving inappropriately. If the teacher spent her time and energy on changing the student's inappropriate behavior rather than on adjusting to it, then everyone would benefit. However, because the teacher believes that the student is possessed, it is not reasonable for her to tell the student to behave or to make the student behave appropriately.

As the teacher further explores this belief-system of possession, she asks herself, "What is the prognosis for cure? What are the chances of this student's being successful in school? Is he going to be cured by tomorrow, by next week, by the end of the semester? How long?" Of course, she doesn't really know the answer (given her belief in possession), but it is clear that she is not the agent of change.

The logic and the questioning-method behind the analysis of this particular belief-system can be applied to any belief-system which predisposes the responsible adult to see the student as being incapable of self-control. The adult must look for evidence to support her belief. Again, if she finds evidence which supports the contention that the student is capable of doing what she wants, then her belief-system of incapability must be inaccurate.

Belief in the student's incapability will affect an adult's way of perceiving him, communicating with him, and acting toward him. Even though most people can see the logic in this analysis of the belief in possession, when they consider other, more widely popular belief-systems—including the so-called "sacred cows" of education and of psychology—they tend to lose sight of this same logic. It is important to understand the process of analysis before scrutinizing these "sacred cows".

Again, possession was used here to demonstrate that once a responsible adult accepts a particular belief, then certain consequences will follow. To help her student to be successful, she must look for evidence to support her belief. If she finds such evidence—whether her belief be in possession, hyperactivity, or one of the other systems to be presented below—then she must do whatever is necessary and congruent with that belief-system in order to make the student successful. If, on the other hand, she finds evidence which contradicts her beliefs, then she must change her belief-system.

## Heredity

Many people are convinced that behavior is a result of heredity. If the student's behavior results from a genetic predisposition, the chances of changing his behavior are even more remote than if he were possessed by the Devil. If the behavior is hereditary, what would a teacher or a parent have to do to change that student's behavior? Change the genes and chromosomes? Do intracellular microscopic genetic transplants to change the genes? Scientists are doing fantastic work in the genetic area, but can they determine which gene it is that causes someone to set fires, to lose his homework, to throw milk cartons at the vice-principal, or to cuss at the teacher? Which is the gene for cussing? How does that gene work?

When responsible adults really do believe that inappropriate behavior is hereditary, then it is important to question the validity of their belief-system. A school counselor might question a parent in this way: "I understand that he is cussing at the teacher, rolling around on the floor, and throwing milk cartons in school. Tell me; does he do the same things in your home? Does he cuss at his dad? Does he cuss at you? Does he cuss at the vice-principal? Does he cuss at the cop? Does he cuss at the minister of the church? He has six teachers; why does he cuss at only one teacher? If it is genetically caused, how does he control his cussing under these various circumstances? How does that work? Does he have genes that allow him to cuss out only certain people? How do the genes tell the difference between these various people and various situations? How can he control his behavior here—but not there? Explain that to me."

Responsible adults must examine the evidence to support the contention that genetic factors cause inappropriate school behaviors. More often than not, they will find ample evidence that the student is capable of controlling himself.

Interestingly, most parents and teachers don't come right out and say, "Well, I think it is hereditary." Rather, they say, "He is just like his dad."

Under these circumstances, the counselor must ask, "Do you mean that he is just like his dad because it is genetically determined? Or do you mean that he loves his dad so much that he wants to be just like him, and that he learns his behavior from him?"

Most people favor the learning model over the genetic model. Sometimes, however, people really believe that the behavior is genetically determined, particularly in such areas as learning disabilities or mental illness. They say, "He is just like his dad. His dad couldn't read or write either, so it's got to be genetic."

There might be some truth to this contention, but, again, the counselor must ask the parent or the teacher for proof. What evidence exists to support this position? Can the genetic factors be overridden with appropriate learning and education?

A special-education teacher in New York state described a student whom she perceived as "genetically unable to read". She was sure that the boy's problem was genetic because no one on his father's side of the family could read. When asked what had happened with the boy, she described her program with pride. She worked with that boy, took him under her wing, even made him come in during her conference period every day for individual tutoring in reading. After several years of dedicated efforts by herself and others, the boy passed the state high-school proficiency exams. The teacher is justifiably proud of having spent the time and energy necessary to enable the boy to learn. However, if genetics had been the cause of his inability to learn to read initially, then he never would have been able to learn to read. Her own excellent teaching undermined her belief-system!

There are many students who say that they can't read and write, but nevertheless they have learned how to read and spell cuss words. If they can't read and write, how can they read and spell all those cuss words? If they have learned how to read and write those particular words, then they can learn to read and write other words—especially if they spend the time and the energy necessary to practice. It is not surprising that some youngsters cannot read, write, or spell, given the actual time which they devote to working on these tasks. But students can and do improve their reading and writing skills when they are seen as being capable of doing so, receive proper instruction, and are required to spend the time and energy necessary to learn these vital skills.

## Emotional Problems

Teachers sometimes believe that a student's bad behavior results from deep-seated emotional problems. Few people believe that a student who is emotionally ill can control himself and be cured by next Friday. If the student is really emotionally handicapped, a popular term used in special education, is he going to be cured by the end of the semester, or even by the end of the year?

If the student is emotionally disturbed, is he really in control of his behavior? Will any teacher be able to change him? Will calling in the school counselor or the school psychologist really help the student? Most teachers believe that if a student is emotionally disturbed he needs to see a private psychiatrist. Even with that treatment, how many people really believe that the student will be cured after seeing a psychiatrist for a year?

Remember: once a teacher has adopted a particular belief-system, it affects her perception and interactions with the student. Again, if she believes that Johnny misbehaves because he has emotional problems or suffers from mental illness, she will believe that he is not in control, that she is not the agent of change, and that the prognosis is not good. Is it reasonable for her to get upset with this student, to make him sit down, or to demand that he control himself? Most people would allow the inappropriate behavior to continue because it is consistent with their belief in the student's incapability of change. Based on teachers' beliefs, interaction patterns between teachers and "normal" students and between teachers and those students whom they believe to be "emotionally disturbed" are significantly different.

Consider Ms. Jones's classroom. Alex, one of her straight "A" students (a great kid), comes into the classroom. Unfortunately, Alex has had a bad day. He chases another student into the classroom, knocking a chair over. What is Ms. Jones going to say and do? Probably she'll say something like, "Alex, knock that stuff off. Leave this classroom and come in here like you are supposed to. You know better than that; don't ever do that again." That's a typical interaction pattern with "normal" students. She believes that Alex is capable and should be held accountable for his behavior.

Now suppose that a psychologist comes in and says to Ms. Jones, "Since you are such a dynamic teacher, we're going to give you Johnny, who is just coming back from the mental hospital. He hurt a teacher last year by trying to put the teacher's head through a window. He is doing much better, but he still has an uncontrollable temper. If you say the wrong thing, he might still explode, so be careful." Under these circumstances, Ms. Jones already perceives Johnny differently from the way she views Alex. Let's say that the student has been in Ms. Jones's classroom for a week, without doing anything inappropriate. On a bad day, though, he chases another student into the classroom and knocks a chair over. In other words, he does the same thing which the straight "A" student has done. What does Ms. Jones do and say to him now? She probably says something like, "Are you having a problem today? Do you need to talk to our school psychologist?" No matter what the communication is, she probably will not use the same kind of communication that she would use with a student whom she considers capable of self-control. The message to teachers is clear: Look closely at what you actually do and say.

Although the two situations are similar, the teacher in this example does not say or demand the same things in the two cases. The actual communication patterns which teachers use allow some students to go crazy because clear directives to stop inappropriate behavior are not given. It is important that teachers attend to any inappropriate behavior in the classroom and take an active stance to stop the initial behavior before it begins to look like "crazy" behavior.

Following the tenets of behavior modification, a teacher may decide to ignore such behavior, saying to herself, "Today I'm going to ignore this behavior so that I can extinguish it. I'm going to reinforce only appropriate behavior." However, if she follows this course of action—or non-action—she will lose control of students who are acting out. If she ignores the behavior, her students will be tearing the place apart within 15 minutes.

It is interesting that when the student escalates his misbehavior beyond the teacher's tolerance level, she says something like, "Knock it off! Sit down in your seat right now, and I mean it!" Ninety percent of the time, the student then stops the inappropriate behavior and sits in his seat. Although she "couldn't" stop the behavior at Step One when it started, she is able to stop the behavior after it has escalated to Step Ten.

Why does she wait until she is at Step Ten and angry at the student? Why doesn't she stop the inappropriate behavior at Step One? There is no reason to allow any inappropriate behavior. If she has a troubled youngster in her classroom and she ignores his inappropriate behavior, then she is giving him a clear message to continue performing the inappropriate behavior.

The movie *Kramer vs. Kramer* provides a good example of ignoring inappropriate behavior. The movie depicts a divorced father and his young son going through some adjustments as they start their new life together. At the dining-room table the child says, in effect, "I'm not eating this garbage. I don't want to eat this junk; I'm going to get some ice cream." Dad, who is sitting next to him, says, "Don't you get up from this table and get that ice cream. If you do, I'm going to spank you." The child says, "Big deal!" and gets up and walks away. The father, two feet away, says, "Don't go over to that refrigerator." Then he says, "Don't pull that chair up; don't open that refrigerator door; don't get that ice cream down; don't stick the spoon in the ice cream; don't stick that spoon in your mouth." At this point the dad gets mad and walks over, spanks the boy, and sends him to bed.

This sequence illustrates the consequences of allowing inappropriate behavior to escalate to Step Ten before stopping it. The father could have stopped the behavior before it escalated and, more importantly, before he hit his son.

A little while later, as they talk, the real issues become apparent. The boy looks at his dad and says, "Dad, if I do terrible and awful things, are you going to leave me like Mom did?" Suddenly the dad realizes that all of this inappropriate behavior was the child's way of finding out where he fits in the family and whether or not he can count on the parent.

Dad says, "No, I wouldn't leave you. You are part of this family, and we are going to stay together." The child then knows that he can count on his dad to be a parent and to provide guidance rather than punishment. The point is that Dad could have stopped his son at Step One instead of waiting until Step Ten, when he spanked the child. When the boy said, "I'm not eating this garbage" and stood up to go toward the ice cream, Dad could have stood up with him, taken him by the shoulders, and said, "No, son, you're not getting ice cream. Let me help you sit down. Now if you don't want to eat your dinner, that is okay; but if you choose not to eat your dinner, then there is no ice cream. I won't beat you or punish you, but I will prevent you from getting any ice cream."

Parents and teachers may wonder why the child persisted when he knew that he was going to get into trouble. He continued the behavior for several reasons: First, the father gave him the choice by not giving clear directives. Second, the father ignored inappropriate behavior by not stopping it at Step One, in effect telling the child to keep going. Third, the child wanted to know where he fit in, and whether or not the father would take control and offer him guidance.

All children need direction, guidance, and structure. When children are given no guidance whatsoever, either in a family setting or in a classroom, trouble will develop within an hour or two. Initially, children need clear directions, consistent messages, guidance, and structure so that they know where they fit in. If they have a sense of where they fit in, they feel better about themselves, are less anxious, feel more comfortable in the world, and can get on in a more positive way with the business of learning, growing, and developing. After they have experienced this structure for some time, they internalize the process and become more self-regulated.

Consider these examples in challenging the belief of emotional illness. A certain junior high school had a self-contained classroom for emotionally disturbed youngsters which deserved its "battle zone" reputation. Each of the 12 children in this classroom was called in for an initial interview with the school psychologist. One particular boy was asked, "Why do you think that you are in this class?" (This youngster had tried to beat up an elementary-school teacher and had attempted to throw her through a window.) He replied, "I tried to hurt the teacher and they just didn't understand me, so they thought I had to be in this weird class. I've got this uncontrollable temper. When I get mad, look out. I cuss, throw things, and come out fighting." (This child had clearly internalized his labels: "uncontrollable temper", "crazy", "weird".) His teachers and his parents also agreed that he couldn't control himself and felt that they couldn't control him, either.

The rest of the interview went like this: "Gee, that is really amazing. 'Uncontrollable.' That is really something. You've been at this school for about a month. I know that you are in Physical Education and Shop and that all the rest of your classes are in the self-contained classroom. Tell me, do you have this uncontrollable temper when you are with the P.E. teacher?" (The psychologist knew that this particular P.E. teacher could handle him.)

"Oh, no; that guy is mean. He doesn't put up with anyone messing off."

"So you control yourself there. I see. What about the Shop teacher?"

"No, he is real cool. We have a good time in there."

"So you control yourself there. Very interesting." (In the self-contained class the students were literally putting holes in the walls and tearing the place apart. These 12 students took up the majority of the vice-principal's time.)

"Tell me, do you do this same type of uncontrolled stuff with the vice-principal?"

"No way! That guy is a real red-neck."

"I see. So you don't do it with the P.E. teacher, the Shop teacher, or the vice-principal. Interesting. What about in the E.H. [Emotionally Handicapped] self-contained classroom? How do you act and what do you do when you're in there?" (Long story illustrating all his uncontrollable inappropriate behavior.) "Well... do you have an uncontrollable temper at home?"

"Oh, yeah. I throw things, break things, and cuss, if that's what you mean."

"Tell me, do you do the exact same things with your dad and your mom?"

"Oh, no; my dad is a child-abuser."

"What do you mean?"

"If I cussed like that at him, he'd punch my lights out."

"How many times have you cussed out your dad?"

"Not too often."

"So you don't do the same things with your dad that you do with your mom? What do you do when you get upset with your mother?"

"I cuss, yell, and throw and break things."

"What do you break?"

"I break anything and everything around."

"Do you break the TV set?"

"Oh, no; I like to watch TV."

"Do you break your mother's best china?"

"You kidding? If I touched that, she'd kill me."

"I see."

By now it is apparent that this kid is in control. He knows whom to get mad with; he knows whom to cuss at; he knows what to break, where to break it, and when to break it. He does not have "an uncontrollable temper". Probably when he started this pattern of "uncontrollable" behavior as a child (Step One) everybody backed away and gave him no clear directives to stop the behavior. Soon he escalated the misbehavior by banging, yelling, screaming, cussing, and breaking things (Step Ten), and people still backed away from him.

So now, twelve years later, the teacher and the parents believe that the child cannot control himself. It is particularly tragic that the child internalizes this belief and labels himself uncontrollable. In fact, most special-education students—especially the ones in junior high or high school self-contained classes—have labeled themselves weird, strange, crazy, or different. At some level these students believe that they are different, and they act accordingly. When a child or a student begins to act "weird", he should be stopped immediately and prevented from going to "Step Ten". It is a disservice to the child to have adults back off and allow the inappropriate behavior.

Consider this similar situation. A fourth-grade teacher once described a student as one of the scariest kids whom she had ever known. When he got mad, he just went nuts. His eyes dilated, the veins in his neck stood out, his fists clenched, and he got red in the face. She feared that he would kill somebody someday. She isolated him and left him alone until he calmed down and regained control of himself. She indicated that neither she nor his parents could control him. By backing off, believing that there was nothing that she could do, and letting this student "go nuts" until he got control of himself, she and his parents inadvertently reinforced his inappropriate behavior and his belief that he had an uncontrollable temper. Interestingly enough, even though the teacher felt that she could not make the student control his behavior, she could always make him go to the isolation area and stay there until he "got control of himself".

Another example concerns a student who went from a psychiatric hospital into a small special high school designed for students to work at their own pace. Immediately following the student's first day in class, his English teacher came running into the school office wanting to know all about this youngster's psychological problems and family background. When the counselor asked what had happened, she said that the boy was really scary and that she needed the information in order to understand him and to teach him English. When asked what the boy actually did when he came into her class, she said that he walked in, checked in to the class, sat down, stared off into space, and did nothing. She was asked what she did about that behavior, and she replied that she did nothing because he scared her. As often happens in small schools, the teacher had heard about the student before his arrival. Because of her preconceived notions about someone coming from a mental hospital, she did not direct the student to do his work. The counselor suggested that as a first step she walk over to him, give him an assignment, and tell him to get to work.

When people believe that a student is severely emotionally disturbed, they often back off and let the student act inappropriately. It is up to parents and teachers to challenge the belief-system, so that the student is no longer seen as being incapable. When teachers or parents see a student as being capable of appropriate behavior, then it becomes reasonable to confront any inappropriate behavior and to stop it at "Step One" before it gets out of hand on the way to "Step Ten".

## Emotional Deprivation

Well-meaning adults often consider deprivation to be the cause of student misbehavior. In this particular belief-system, the adult sees the student as having been deprived of some element necessary for his academic, emotional, and/or social well-being: love, affection, status, prestige, attention, or any other element significant to the student's well-being. Many teachers, for instance, believe that Johnny misbehaves because he does not get enough attention. Because Johnny is deprived of love or attention, he sets fires, cusses, acts inappropriately in the classroom, or neglects to do his homework.

A teacher who subscribes to this belief needs to challenge it and find out what evidence she has to support it. Once she actively challenges her belief, she will begin to see that deprivation does not necessarily have anything to do with inappropriate behavior. Hasn't she known some students who seem to get almost anything that they want and still act inappropriately? Has she ever wondered why some students get a lot of attention and yet are brats, while some others who don't get as much attention behave well? What makes the difference? Has she ever known a student who has been deprived through the death of a parent and yet behaves appropriately? What makes the difference? Unquestionably, a person who has been deprived has been hurt, and his feelings are affected. As a teacher, she can work with him and do the best that she can to help him, but she can't use deprivation as an excuse for letting the student act inappropriately, get poor grades, or neglect his homework. Of course she wants to be as sensitive as possible to all of her students' emotional needs. She wouldn't think of giving extra homework to a student whose father has just died. The question is, "How long does she let this student not do his homework or not act appropriately? One week? A year? Ten years?" If she buys into this belief-system, and uses it as an ongoing excuse, then she inadvertently encourages irresponsibility and misbehavior. The student can be deprived and still get good grades and (one hopes) makes something of himself in the future, or he can be deprived and get F's and go on welfare for the rest of his life. Which route would she prefer for her student? The teacher needs to ask herself how a deprived student controls himself on certain days, for certain periods of time, under various situations, or with certain people. If he is able to control himself under some circumstances, she doesn't need to accept any excuse for his not behaving appropriately under all circumstances.

If the teacher believes that Johnny misbehaves because he is emotionally deprived, what would she need to do to get him to act more appropriately? She would have to make up for all the love and attention which he has missed during his entire life before she could expect him to do his homework and act appropriately in her classroom. But will she have the time to give him what he seems to require? If she gives him a high percentage of her personal time and energy, will it be enough? Or will he need even more? It's not that children don't need love and attention—they do, and it is my belief that the teacher should give all of her students as much love and attention as she can give. However, the point is that giving or not giving attention to them does not necessarily get them to do their homework and to act appropriately in class. While she gives them as much love and attention as possible, the teacher must also expect them to achieve and to behave appropriately. Love, by itself, is not enough. Many parents clearly love their children but expect little and demand little in terms of appropriate behavior and school achievement. Perhaps the optimal condition combines love with high expectation.

## Ignorance

Some teachers believe that a student does not really understand the consequences of his behavior, the implications of his actions, or the significance of society's behavioral norms. Such a belief assumes that the student is ignorant and does not know what is expected of him. He is seen as not understanding the rules and "complexities" of home, school, and society. This belief in the student's ignorance implies that he can't be expected to behave or to be held responsible for his behavior. Since the student "doesn't understand", both teachers and parents try to teach the student over and over again what he should do and how he should behave.

What parents and teachers say and do reflects what they believe. Sometimes adults say things such as, "That kid is firing on only half a cylinder", or "Go to school and learn something, stupid." Both statements are clearly giving the student the message that he is ignorant. Often adults say only indirectly that the child is ignorant. Statements like "You have to *learn* to sit still;" "You have to *learn* not to hit Susie"; and "You have to *learn* the rules of this school because society has rules and regulations. You can't just go around doing what you want to do" imply that the student is stupid and doesn't know the rules or how to perform the preferred behavior. In either case, for the adults to speak in this fashion to a child presupposes that they see the child as being incapable of doing what is expected of him and in all probability is stupid or ignorant because he doesn't "know" any better.

Any direct or indirect comment about the child's assumed ignorance should be challenged: "When he has to *learn* to bring his papers and pencils to class, does that mean that he doesn't know how to do that right now? Is he capable of bringing his papers and pencils to class? Has he ever brought his papers and pencils to school before? Is he stupid? Does he really not understand that if he does not bring his books and his work to class that he will fail?"

Probably he knows how to do whatever is requested of him; he has done it in the past, and he understands the rules. Past behavior implies that he knows how to do whatever is requested. He is not stupid, and he doesn't really need to learn how to do the required behavior. He already has the skills; he is capable. All that remains is for him to do it.

It is amazing that this concept of incapability is applied to such simple behaviors as "learning" to sit still or "learning" to bring books to class. Very young children can sit still; yet we develop a highly complex belief that some high-school students can't sit still for a minute.

What evidence exists to support such a belief? If the parent or teacher has ever seen him sit still for over a minute, then he is capable of sitting still. If the student got to class on time throughout junior high school, then he is capable of getting to class on time even if he is now being late for class. However, for some reason many people ignore evidence that is contrary to their belief, and therefore they continue to believe that the student doesn't know how to sit still or how to get to class on time.

### Brain Damage

The idea of brain damage provides another belief-system. In this particular belief we see the student's behavior as resulting from neurological impairment or from minimal brain dysfunction. While brain damage and minimal brain dysfunction do exist in some cases, it is important to question how and whether the brain damage relates to the behavior in question. Often doctors' and psychologists' reports indicate brain damage in many youngsters who act appropriately in school. Conversely, many "normal" junior-high-school students act in a highly inappropriate manner—all of which leads one to question the validity of this belief in relation to specific behaviors.

Teachers and parents need to ask themselves, or perhaps to ask the child's doctor, some simple questions: "What part of the brain is dysfunctional? What evidence do you have to support your position? How does this brain damage affect his cursing only at the third-period teacher or failing to do his homework?" In challenging any belief based on the neurology or physiology of the child, one would ask the same simple questions: "Does he curse all teachers, the vice-principal, the principal, both the mother and the father, the minister? Has he done his homework before? Under what circumstances? If so, how has he done the behavior here, there, or under other circumstances, if he is brain-damaged?" If he has done it before, then he is capable of doing what is expected, and brain damage has nothing to do with the particular behavior. Again, look for the evidence.

Although in some cases brain damage does exist, and brain damage can indeed affect behavior, brain damage usually affects behavior in fairly specific ways. Children with some form of minimal brain dysfunction or even retardation behave appropriately in well-run special-education classrooms. Yet "normal" junior-high-school students in ordinary classrooms often behave inappropriately. If evidence exists that a particular student can control himself, then brain damage has nothing to do with his inappropriate behavior.

A high-school principal requested that a psychologist see a student immediately. He said that a girl in the self-contained classroom was snorting, banging her head against the wall, and acting like a pig. The psychologist went to the high school self-contained classroom and found the girl behind the time-out screen, curled up in a semi-fetal position. This girl had previously been hospitalized for a "psychotic episode". In a kind but firm tone of voice, the psychologist told the girl to get up and go to the counseling office. The psychologist and the girl walked to the office and sat down. Once there, she looked away and started banging her head and snorting. The psychologist reached over, took her head, turned it toward himself, and said, "No more snorting. Look at me when we're talking. You know that I care about you and love you, but I'm not going to put up with that behavior. Now, you are hurting, and right now I'm hurting for you. But I'm no mind-reader. Tell me what is going on."

They talked for about two hours, and it was apparent that she had personal, social, and academic problems. The psychologist involved the family in counseling to prevent her from being sent back to the hospital.

During the counseling session, the psychologist looked for the interaction patterns and the belief-systems within the family. He began to explore with the family what they expected from the girl, what they wanted to be changed, and what needed to be done to help her. One of the parents' top priorities was to get her to wash her face and take a bath. When the psychologist asked why they believed that she didn't wash her face and take a bath, the father replied that it was because she had been brain-damaged since birth. When asked whether his daughter had ever washed her face or taken a bath by herself, the father said that she had done so off and on, whenever she felt like it. The psychologist then asked the father if she had washed her face or taken a bath when he had made her do it.

"Sure," he replied. "But it is a knock-down, drag-out fight to get her to do it. She throws such a temper-tantrum, yells, and screams, you would not believe it."

"If your daughter has been brain-damaged since birth and therefore is incapable of washing her face, then how is it that she has washed her face on her own on several occasions and also every single time that you made her do it—even though it was a knock-down, drag-out fight? How do you explain that she was able to wash her face if she is brain-damaged?"

The daughter may have been brain-damaged, but it was obvious that brain damage had nothing to do with her ability to wash her face or take a bath. The parent had evidence (proof positive) that she was capable of washing her face because she had often done so.

Ultimately, even if the child is brain-damaged, the questions which the teacher or parent must ask remain the same: "Can you let the child continue the inappropriate behavior without taking some measures to prevent that behavior? Is there some way that the child can compensate for the damage and learn to act appropriately?"

### Defective or Inadequate Role Models

The belief in defective or inadequate role models implies that the student's behavior is influenced by bad role models such as parents, teachers, or peer groups. The structure of this belief-system is as follows: Person A is a terrible good-for-nothing who gets poor grades and disrupts his class. The real reason for Person A's behavior, however, is that Person B—an inadequate role model—is making him do it.

In a school situation, what options does a teacher have in changing Student A if, in fact, it is Student B who is causing him to act inappropriately? The only options are to change Student B or to move Student B—preferably out of state. Unfortunately, Student A always seems to find another student to follow inappropriately.

From the parents' perspective, the structure of the problem is the same. The parents will spend their lifetimes trying to shape up everybody else's children and never tell their own child to stop the inappropriate behavior. From their perspective, it is not reasonable to tell their child to stop the inappropriate behavior because they feel that he is being overly influenced by others and can't possibly say "No" to them. It is all those rotten kids, all those bums down the street, who are making him do what he is doing. This clear message conveys to the child that he doesn't have to be responsible for his own behavior because no one expects responsibility from him, and, besides, someone else made him do all those rotten things. Unfortunately, over the years the child internalizes this belief and learns to give the classic response, "I didn't do it; he made me. . . ." The student doesn't have to take responsibility for his own behavior because everybody believes that someone else is making him do it. Somehow, the parents believe that the child is so wishy-washy, so spineless, that he could not possibly say "No" to any undue influence.

To erode this belief-system the counselor needs to question both parents and student. She can ask the student, "When you left school with the other kids, did they have to make you leave campus? Did they drag you off fighting? When you took those drugs, did someone cram them down your throat?"

Most high-school students who are rebellious and in deep trouble usually reply, "Nobody makes me do nothin'!" When asked if they have ever said "No" to anyone who was trying to influence them, they say "Yes!"

The counselor should then ask the parents how they explain that behavior if he is such a follower. Also, she should ask the parents to explain how he got to be such a wishy-washy individual who has no ability to stand up to others. Is he just like Dad? Did he learn his behavior from Mom? Is his behavior genetic? Usually there is quite a lot of evidence to support the fact that the child is in control and is not unduly influenced.

A variation of Person B's unduly influencing Person A's behavior is also found within the family structure. This variation usually takes one of two forms. In the first situation, Dad says to Mom, "If you knew how to discipline the child, we wouldn't have this problem." Here, Mom is the bad role-model, and Dad usually spends most of his time trying to convince her to change instead of telling the child to behave. The counselor needs to redirect the focus. She might ask the father how long he has been trying to change his wife.

"For fifteen years," he might reply.

"Has it worked?"

"No."

"Well, since we have only about a semester left of school, and I assume that she is not going to change much in the next few months, is there anything that you would like to tell your son about going to school?"

The second situation is from the wife's point-of-view. She tells the husband that if he took an interest in his kids and spent a little more time with them instead of working all the time or playing golf with his buddies, they wouldn't be having all this trouble. In this variation, Dad becomes the bad role-model. Here the counselor might ask the wife whether she has known any fathers who were away more and whose kids didn't act this way. Has she ever known any families in which the father was dead and in which the kids didn't act this way? How about divorced and single-parent homes? Has she ever known any families in which the father was very much involved and in which the child still acted inappropriately? How can these situations be explained if, in fact, the father's absence is what causes the child to act inappropriately?

This Inadequate Role-Model belief-system of some parents, with Person B influencing Person A, has even been extended to include teachers and school personnel. Parents say that their child avoids school because schools are "too goody-goody", "too abstract", "too ivory-tower", "too easy", "too hard", "too boring", or "too irrelevant". (Teachers are poor role-models; therefore, they cause the child to be truant and to fail in school.)

Other variations of this belief include such things as the teacher's poor personality, lack of a sense of humor, or lack of dedication. When any of these variations comes up, ask "Even if that is true, is it okay for your child not to do his homework ever again? Is it okay for him to flunk out of school? Even if what you say is true, why do you believe that your son can't act appropriately and do his homework? I don't know about you, but I sat through a few classes, did my homework, and acted appropriately even though I personally thought that the teacher had 'no personality' and 'no sense of humor'." The point is that it would be nice if all teachers were great and if all students loved them, loved school, and did their homework cheerfully. But if not all teachers are as good as all of that, does this fact provide a good enough reason for a child never to do school work again or to act inappropriately?

Raising a child may indeed be much more difficult if the role-models around him are not everything that one could hope for, but parents should not permit those shortcomings to become an excuse for allowing the child to act inappropriately. If the child is to overcome some of these "poor models" and to become successful in life, then parents and teachers must expect him to control himself and to be responsible for his own actions.

### Socio-economic Status

If defective models cannot be used as an excuse, neither can socio-economic status (S.E.S.) be used as an excuse. In today's world it is a fairly popular belief that one can't expect much from children who come from poor backgrounds. It is clear that S.E.S. does affect people's lives. A large body of research-findings indicates that S.E.S. is highly correlated with numerous educational and personal outcome measures, from school grades to persistence to self-concept. However, if low S.E.S. causes students to fail, how does one explain the many economically poor students who not only survive but actually do well? There are also students from high S.E.S. groups who have poor grades and who act inappropriately. How does one explain that fact using this belief-system as an excuse? If teachers and parents allow themselves to use S.E.S. as an excuse to permit students to get out of doing the work, then it is very likely that the students will *not* do the work. Since development of skills provides an avenue for success and allows students who come from families with low S.E.S. to rise above poverty and limited human potential, teachers and parents should expect all children to do well and, thereby, widen their horizons and their opportunities to succeed. Teachers need to do everything in their power to make children do well so that they can rise above their poverty and low socio-economic status.

## Phases and Stages of Development

Parents and teachers often tolerate a child's inappropriate behavior because they believe that he is simply going through a phase or stage of development. Usually, but not always, there is an implication of genetic determination that somehow controls these stages of development. A father once said that his junior-high-school son was fighting at school because he was going through secondary sex changes. When the counselor asked how this particular stage of his son's development caused him to fight, the father explained that the problem was hormonal. The counselor pointed out that 80-90% of that junior high school's males were going through secondary sex changes, yet only two had had fights that year. If secondary sex changes are the cause of fights, then why were there so few fights?

The counselor needs to question parents and teachers whenever she suspects that the "reason" for inappropriate behavior is phases, stages, or genetic determination. Some standard inquiries, depending on the situation, might be: "Show me the genetically determined phase or stage of development for cussing, not doing homework, or hitting your sister. If this is a genetically or non-genetically determined phase, how do you explain it? Do all children go through this phase? All children from the same culture, same religion, same race, same socio-economic group? How do you explain the differences in children if this is a phase that all children go through? If he grows out of this phase, how will you explain the change?"

Consider what people do and say when they believe that a particular behavior is a stage of development: Two mothers take their two-year-old sons to the grocery store. Both toddlers are trying to destroy the store by pulling items off the shelves. One mother believes that it's the "terrible two's". The other mother believes that the child is acting inappropriately and takes a firm stance to prevent the child from acting up. Both mothers might initially have difficulty with their child; both might be embarrassed by the scenes in the store. However, one mother will probably be putting up with this and similar behaviors for the rest of her life, while the second mother will be giving her child a clear message that she will not tolerate inappropriate behavior. She will, in a relatively short period of time, have a well-behaved youngster who realizes that no matter what the setting, he is expected to behave appropriately. The second mother may have to back up her demand for appropriate behavior for a period of time and in many different settings, but her belief that the child is capable of appropriate behavior enables her to demand and eventually to get appropriate behavior.

Adults act differently when they believe that the child is "just going through a stage." Even when confronted with evidence to the contrary, some parents and some teachers still believe that "it is just a stage." To erode this belief, the counselor can ask a series of pointed questions: "How long is this stage going to last? When will he be expected to grow out of this stage and act appropriately? How will you explain this change in behavior when it happens?" Interestingly, when the parents expect that the child "should" grow out of a particular stage (*e.g.,* bed-wetting, hyperactivity, not doing his homework), the child generally does behave appropriately within three or four months of the target date.

### Natural or Normal Behavior

Very similar to the Phases and Stages of Development belief is the belief that inappropriate behavior is natural. In this case, parents and/or teachers may say, "This is just the way children are; boys will be boys"; "That's the way I grew up"; "That's the way it is in my family"; or "Kids are just like that; they aren't meant to sit still for more than a minute. They need to get up and run off all that energy." If an adult believes that such behavior is natural, she will allow the behavior to continue even though she might not like it. She might even feel that it is inappropriate to try to stop the behavior since one can't oppose the true nature of things. This belief is one of the reasons why some teachers do not systematically apply techniques which they know work to other areas in which they are having difficulty with the students. For example, some teachers feel that correcting misbehavior goes against the student's nature.

If this truly is natural behavior, do all children do it? If not, how does one account for the difference? "Boys will be boys." All boys? All cultures? All races? All religions? "Children need to run off all that energy every fifteen minutes." All children? All geographical areas? All cultures?

Examine "normal" language at schools today. Kindergarten teachers describe kids who cuss better than sailors. What do these teachers do when they hear profanity? Often, they don't take an active stance to stop the behavior because "that's just normal behavior" and "everyone" is doing it. What can anyone expect or do about it?

Teachers and parents must first see a particular behavior as a problem and then want to change it. It may be necessary to convince them that they have the power to do something about it.

In a session with a divorced mother and her sixteen-year-old son, the son told the mother that she was full of s____ . The mother appeared upset by this language, but she didn't say anything to her son about it. She sat in her chair, thought it over for a few seconds, and said, "Well, at least now you know how he acts at home. He's shown his true colors. This is just the tip of the iceberg."

When asked if her son's language was a problem that she would like to change, she indicated that there was nothing she could do because she herself cussed ("normal behavior").

"Then it's no problem that your son talks to you that way. What else would you like to talk about?"

"Well, it *is* a problem because I'm his mother, and I don't like it."

"Perhaps you can do something about it and tell him never to cuss at you again."

"No, I couldn't do that."

"Okay; no problem. Then just forget it and let him talk to you that way and live with it for the rest of your life."

"Well, I can't do that, either, because it really bugs me."

"Fine. Then do something about it."

Finally, after a few more minutes of this type of logic, she got the message that her son's disrespectful language actually was a problem to her and that she could take a stance to change the behavior.

Parents and teachers often believe that they are powerless to change any behavior which they believe to be "normal". Once this belief has been eroded, however, they are free to decide whether or not they wish to make a stand and clearly demand a change in any behavior which they find intolerable.

### Hyperactivity

Many people subscribe to the belief that inappropriate behavior is the result of hyperactivity. This belief is one of the sacred cows of current education and one to which many people have a strong emotional commitment. When someone swears that her child or student is hyperactive, the counselor needs to ask for the evidence that exists to prove it. (Although there must be some hyperactive children in the world, I have not found one parent or teacher who has been able to prove that her child's inappropriate behavior was the result of hyperactivity or who has not been able to control his behavior.) The counselor should ask the teacher or parent to describe the behavior first in very specific, concrete terms and then to explain what causes the unacceptable behavior. Bio-chemistry? Blood-sugar level? Neurological impairments? Minimal brain damage? Phases of the moon?

The counselor could then ask a teacher, "Does he ever sit still? Under what circumstances? Does he act the same way with all of his junior high teachers? Does he act the same way when the principal walks into the room? Does he act the same way when you get angry and tell him to sit still?" Or if the counselor is speaking to parents, "Does he act the same way at home? While watching T.V.? At your dining-room table? While his father is there? His mother? The grandparents? The minister, priest, or rabbi? The police? Does he act the same way in church? In court? Does he act the same way on the week-ends? During summer vacation?"

As the counselor gathers information on his behavior, it usually becomes very apparent that the child acts differently under different circumstances within short time-intervals. How is it that the child is hyperactive in only first, third, and sixth periods at school if it is the blood-sugar level that causes him to be hyperactive? Does he have two different types of physiological systems, one to turn the blood-sugar level on and one to turn it off? How did he control himself when the principal was there? The father? The policeman?

After a while the child begins to believe and accept the label of "hyperactive". Students occasionally tell teachers that they don't have to behave because they forgot to take their medication for hyperactivity.

Once the child starts to believe that he can't control himself, it is unreasonable to expect that he will act in appropriate ways. How can one expect a child to sit still when everyone, including the child, believes that he is hyperactive?

The problem is that after ten years of this inappropriate behavior, it becomes very difficult for some of us to find evidence to the contrary and believe in the child's capabilities. However, some contradictory evidence probably does exist if one looks closely enough. In fact, sometimes the evidence is so obvious that even the "experts" overlook it.

A teacher once described a little girl who was the worst hyperactive child that she or the school had ever had. This girl was such a problem that everyone in the school (teachers, bus driver, noon aides) knew all about her even though they might not have had her in class. After trying unsuccessfully to deal with her behavior, school personnel decided to hold a School Assessment Team (S.A.T.) meeting to talk with the parents about the possibility of special education. At this meeting the school brought in all the experts, including the school nurse, speech therapist, psychologist, principal, teachers, and just about everyone else who had ever had any contact with the child. The school personnel wanted to impress upon the parents the severity of the problem and the child's need for special help. The S.A.T. meeting was one of the longest meetings which the school had ever had, lasting over two-and-one-half hours. During the meeting, the members of the S.A.T. team said such things as: "She is so hyper that she can't possibly sit still for more than two minutes"; "She should have a neurological and medical examination with the possibility of getting some medication to see if that might help to control her"; and "The parents should check her diet and her sugar intake to determine if that has some bearing on the problem."

Only after the psychologist's presentation did the teacher realize that the little girl had sat through that entire two-and-a-half-hour meeting without ever once acting inappropriately. The evidence was right there in front of all those experts, but no one saw it. If the child sat still for two and a half hours, then she could sit still longer than two minutes. She did not need a neurological examination to determine whether or not she had a neurological-delay deficit requiring pharmacological interventions, and her blood-sugar level had little or nothing to do with her ability to control herself.

Students have come in to group sessions after "nutrition break", cramming Ding-Dongs down their throats and with cookies in their right pockets and Twinkies in their left, saying "Don't tell my Dad I eat this stuff, because I'm on a special sugar-free diet, and he thinks I get hyper if I eat this stuff."

When a student is asked why he acts inappropriately only in specific periods, such as the first, fourth, or fifth, and not in other periods of the day, he generally replies, "Because the other teachers won't let me."

## Wind and Weather

Another belief is that wind and weather cause the student to act inappropriately. This belief, coupled with the belief that the student's true nature is to run off "all that energy", causes teachers to say, "If it rains for more than two days, we can't possibly control the students because of all that pent-up energy. They get real 'squirrely'."

In the Los Angeles area many teachers believe that they can't control their students when the wind blows in off the desert. The students get restless, and some teachers feel that then they can't teach them anything. Although the hot dry winds must affect the students and the teachers physiologically, one still needs to question how that effect causes cussing, setting fires in the trash cans in the boys' restrooms, or failing to do homework. Under the same conditions, most students continue to behave appropriately. How does one explain that fact? Can those students who act inappropriately manage to control themselves while the principal is in the classroom? If conditions of wind and weather cause students to misbehave, shouldn't all students, or at least the majority, misbehave as long as those weather conditions persist?

One teacher, a stereotypical Mid-Western schoolmarm of 63, loved her kids, but because she was skilled and highly professional, expected them to learn, to act appropriately, and to work. One could walk into her classroom on any school day and at any time, and see the exact same thing—children doing their school work. Rain, snow, and wind made no difference; she expected those children to learn, and they did. Even those students who (other teachers felt) were limited did their work neatly and correctly and without causing a ruckus. In the same school other teachers had difficulty under "poor weather conditions". Of course, the obvious scientific conclusion is that the poor wind-and-weather conditions never reached the schoolmarm's room.

Any teacher can avoid the trap of having weather conditions dictate how students behave by asking herself, "Do all children act this way? If there were a fire drill right now, could these children control themselves? If the principal walked in, could these children get themselves under control? Do all children under these weather conditions act this way?" If she had seen a particular student control himself under these weather conditions before, then he is capable of doing so, and she can insist that he behave appropriately.

## Holidays

The idea that students have trouble behaving themselves during certain times of the day, the week, or the year is another prevalent belief. Some teachers believe that during the last five minutes of the day, the last day of the week, or the last week before any major holiday or vacation it is impossible to control the students. One teacher said, "You may as well play games the last week before Christmas, because the kids are so excited that they can't learn." Teachers who believe that students are capable and who expect them to behave have better results under all circumstances.

## Demanding Too Much of Students

Demanding too much of the student is often believed to have deleterious effects on him; therefore, some educators and parents will not expect much from him and will let him "work at his own pace". This belief has had a tremendous negative effect on American education. At its extreme, this belief suggests that expecting too much causes frustration and anxiety, and can lead to poor academic performance, loss of motivation, and diminished self-concept.

Many worthwhile learning experiences are initially frustrating and difficult. Few new tasks are mastered on the first try. Learning to walk, to ride a bike, to read and write, to play tennis, to type on a word-processor are all initially very frustrating. But after the learner struggles with the tasks, putting more time and energy into them, he begins to be less frustrated and to have more fun.

Many educators no longer expect and demand excellence of their students. Clearly, there are many exceptions in which certain schools and certain individual teachers demand, expect, and get excellent academic performance and fully acceptable social behavior. However, in general, educational standards and expectations are lower today partially as a result of the belief that students should not be unduly frustrated. There are tremendous individual differences in students, and often there are special conditions and circumstances that need to be taken into consideration; however, it is not necessary to lower reasonable minimal standards to accommodate these special needs. Helen Keller, with all her handicapping conditions, had very severe special needs. Luckily for her and luckily for us, she had a teacher who did not lower her expectations in order to spare her student anxiety and frustration.

When teachers work in the field of learning-disabilities, with its emphasis on individualizing instruction, working at the individual's own pace, and motivating students with games and with readiness skills, they sometimes lower their expectations for these students. Often they allow their students to spend less time than other students spend at a given task or to attend a shortened school day. However, if students haven't mastered a task that is deemed important, it is imperative to increase the amount of time devoted to the task rather than to reduce it. Students have never gone crazy as a result of realistically high expectations. They have gone crazy because sometimes those expectations exist in an environmental context of fear, hatred, hostility, shame, and/or guilt. Students who are expected to do well in a context of encouragement, love, and positive worth become highly skilled, competent people who feel good about their skills and about themselves.

The high-school student who cannot read and write is a very hurt, angry youngster who feels that he is stupid. He may require special teaching methods and a systematic curriculum to learn more efficiently, but the major criterion for success is how much time he spends on task. It is hardly surprising that so many high school students are behind in their academic skills, given the brief time which they allot for reading or for doing their homework. If students are expected to do 20 problems, the teacher should not lower her expectation to 10 problems for the students who have difficulty in order that they can work at their own pace. Instead, she should increase the task to 30 or 40 problems so that they can overlearn the concept. In this way they are able to master the necessary skills, to keep up with the rest of the class in skill levels, and to feel good about themselves instead of seeing themselves as dummies. Again, Helen Keller had to put in hours upon hours of extra work just to obtain the "normal" skills necessary to become successful. The professional teacher will skillfully use appropriate teaching methods, curricular materials, and instructional techniques. She will diagnose the student's problem and use task-analysis skills to provide him with the best opportunity to learn. However, given the fact that special instruction and methods may be required, probably the most important variable beyond that is the amount of time which the student spends on the task.

This discussion refers to reasonable expectations; it does not refer to someone with an I.Q. of 50 getting straight A's and becoming a brain surgeon. It refers to realistic observable evidence of capabilities. The problem with attaining mastery is that no one knows what students can do until they spend enough time on task to find out. Students generally have more capabilities than they are given credit for, so sometimes teachers initially have to act on faith. Luckily, Helen Keller's teacher had more faith in Keller's unseen capabilities than Keller's parents did.

A conference speaker once said that during the early 1960s the school district in which he was a principal offered French on an experimental basis at the junior high school. They believed that they could offer this "difficult" subject only to very bright students with I.Q.s of 110 or above. "Imagine my surprise," he said, "when I was in Switzerland some time later and it suddenly dawned on me that everyone there—even people with I.Q.s of far less than 110—spoke at least three languages, one of which was French." Obviously, the Swiss are not afraid to challenge students.

The point is that teachers can expect and demand excellence of their students when they are not deceived by a belief that normal frustration and anxiety are necessarily harmful. Teachers should have realistic expectations, but they should not underestimate anyone's capabilities.

## School Environment

Educational literature is replete with articles on how certain aspects of school environments affect students. Research has been done on such things as schools with or without windows, open or closed classrooms, team teaching, fluorescent lighting, various colors of wall paint, number of students per square foot of floor space, and the effects of various room temperatures on student performance.

Although all of these things surely have some impact on students, how do any of these variables cause a student to cuss in class, roll around on the floor, or refuse to do school work? Again, one must ask the same set of simple questions that have appeared throughout this chapter. Then, if one finds evidence that the student is capable of controlling his behavior under the particular environmental conditions, it is reasonable to expect appropriate behavior.

## Summary

Once parents, teachers, administrators, and counselors become familiar with this simple but effective method of analyzing common beliefs, they will be better able to deal with student behavior problems. They will learn to recognize and deal with a variety of beliefs which sometimes become excuses for letting children misbehave:

The only-child syndrome
The only girl in a family of boys
The only boy in a family of girls
The middle-child syndrome
A change-of-life baby
Divorce/single-parent home
Both parents working
Neither parent working
The child was born "lazy", "bad", "shy", etc.
The adopted child
The illegitimate child
Astrology (born under the wrong sun sign)

Bad long-term habit (hard to change)
Limited potential
Family too strict
Family too permissive
Family too mobile (unsettled)
Welfare-cycle-syndrome child
Student-folder syndrome (excessive faith in entries in cumulative folder)
Early failure (no hope for future performance)
The curse of odd-numbered ages (3,5,7, etc.)
Child fantasizes too much
Misunderstood child
Teacher incompetence
Child too smart for the curriculum (he's bored)
Child disliked by teacher and classmates
Not the teacher's pet

In all of these and many similar beliefs, one needs to apply the same set of simple questions and logic to discover whether or not they are reasonable excuses for inappropriate behavior.

One looks for evidence to substantiate a belief. If there is evidence, one confirms the belief and does the best that she can do to deal with the problem. If the evidence is not there, one changes her views regarding reasons for the student's misbehavior and sees the student as capable, and then expects him to do what is required of him.

Here are several questions which the teacher might ask herself when she considers whether or not to allow a student to continue to misbehave:

(1) Would you let your own child behave this way in class? If not, then do not let any student behave that way in your class.

(2) If the principal sat down beside the student, could the student control himself? While it's frustrating for the teacher when an "acting out" student does not misbehave in front of the principal or the psychologist, it is also a clear indication that the student has control of his behavior. "Hyperactive" students often stop dead in their tracks when the principal walks in. Again, if they can control themselves in a given situation, then they are capable of doing so, and the belief that they can't control themselves is inaccurate.

(3) If you offered the student $1,000 to stop what he is doing or to start doing what you want him to do, could he do it? If so, then the behavior is within the student's control. When high-school students who were flunking out of school were asked, "If I had unlimited resources and promised you one million dollars and a high-school diploma if you come to school every day, get to class on time, and make straight C's for this next semester, do you think you could do it?", only two students said that they couldn't do it—and they were

both gifted students with I.Q.s over 132 who quickly realized that if they said "Yes" the game was up. The rest of the students all indicated that they could do it. Even the "dumb" ones said that they could do it.

(4) Have you ever seen the student do what you want him/her to do— even once? If the student has done it once, then he/she is capable of doing it again.

When a teacher considers popular educational beliefs about why students behave as they do, she has to ask herself, "Does the belief-system perceive the student to be capable of doing what I want, or does the belief-system imply that the student is incapable of controlling himself?" The ultimate way to determine if the student is capable is by gathering evidence. If she has ever seen the student do what she wants him to do, then he is indeed capable of doing it, and she can forget all of the excuses that she had previously entertained. Ultimately, she must accept no unfounded excuses for the student to act inappropriately.

# Chapter III: Ineffective Communication Patterns

Chapter II establishes that unfounded belief-systems about why students misbehave abound. Since what people say is a reflection of what they believe, and since the words which they use reflect their feelings, thoughts, and beliefs, these faulty belief-systems cause teachers to communicate and to behave in ways that are not effective in stopping most inappropriate behavior in the classroom. This chapter will explore and analyze what teachers actually say and do when a student acts inappropriately. It will become apparent that when the teacher believes that the student is incapable of doing what is requested, she uses vague, abstract, and indirect communication patterns. These communications, which correspond with her belief that the student is incapable of controlling himself, by their very nature tell the student to continue acting inappropriately.

## Ignoring Inappropriate Behavior

Ignoring inappropriate behavior and reinforcing appropriate behavior are promoted as effective intervention techniques by advocates of Behavior Modification. Many teachers have been trained and encouraged to use this approach to stop inappropriate behavior in the classroom. This communication method, however, believes that ignoring inappropriate behavior actually encourages the inappropriate behavior to continue instead of extinguishing it, and clearly communicates to the student that it is okay to keep behaving inappropriately. Although Behavior Modification does work with some students who are willing to go along with the program of reinforcement, it rarely works with difficult and unwilling discipline problems. Apparently, for these students, ignoring the behavior clearly implies approval; to them it means that it is okay to act inappropriately, that the teacher does not expect them to behave, and that she believes that they are incapable of behaving.

Students, after all, are just ordinary citizens. If all police officers ignored ordinary citizens going 65 mph, even though the maximum speed limit is 55, what would that tell the speeders? It would tell them that it was okay to go 65 mph. If every police officer ignored those people going 70 mph, what would that tell them? It would tell them that it was okay to go 70. Moreover, if every police officer gives a ticket to all drivers going 71 mph or faster, then it would tell them that it is okay to go 70 mph, but if they exceed 70 mph they will get a ticket.

Students read teachers with radar-like accuracy. They know what is appropriate and what is inappropriate by what teachers actually do and say to stop inappropriate behavior. If teachers stop inappropriate behavior at Step One instead of ignoring it until it gets out of control at Step Ten, they won't have to punish or negatively label their students. Labels, name-calling, hostility, and aggression are unnecessary when inappropriate behavior is stopped before it gets out of hand.

Teachers can understand the effect which adult labels have on students if they try, in a similar fashion, to label themselves. For instance, if a teacher has ever driven over 55 mph, what is she? She is a criminal. In fact, she probably has been a criminal for a long time and has committed multiple offenses. This indicates that she is a chronic offender with sociopathic tendencies—"sociopathic tendencies" because she has no guilt or remorse and therefore doesn't really care about others. This latter statement is based on her poor judgment in light of the common knowledge that anyone who has an accident while driving in excess of 55 mph increases her chances of killing someone else. Therefore, she must not care about others because she continues to exceed the 55-mph speed limit. Besides being a criminal and a sociopath, she has severe emotional problems because when she drives in excess of 55 mph, she not only increases the odds of killing others, but she increases the odds of killing herself as well. She obviously has a deep-seated death wish. But does she see herself as a hardened criminal, a sociopath, a person with severe and deep-seated emotional problems? Probably not. Then why does she continue to break the law? Oh, she can probably come up with some weak excuses: "I was in a hurry." "I needed to get somewhere." "I don't know." "I usually get away with it." Well, students are similar to teachers. When teachers ask students why they misbehave, they come up with similar weak excuses. The difference is that teachers, as adults, reject others' labeling them as criminals and thus are able to maintain relatively good self-images. Children and students, however, have a tendency to accept the labels given to them by significant others, especially if the labeling persists for years.

If the teacher stops the student's inappropriate behavior at Step One, she will not have to label him in a negative way. On the contrary, if she ignores the inappropriate behavior, just like the policeman who ignores speeding motorists, she is telling the student very clearly and specifically that it is okay to continue the inappropriate behavior.

Students need clear directives so that they know where they belong. Both parents and teachers know that if they give absolutely no directions to children in their charge, then they would soon have chaos. Teachers should not ignore *any* inappropriate behavior. Whenever a student goes beyond the limits of appropriate classroom behavior, the teacher must take an active stance to stop the behavior at Step One instead of waiting until Step Ten when the student is out of control. (How to achieve this stopping of bad behavior will be discussed in detail in Chapters V and VI.)

Junior-high and high-school teachers impose a wide variety of limits, and students, moving from class to class, readily adapt to these different limits. To continue the analogy of speed limits, the limit in Ms. X's classes may be 55 mph. In Ms. B's classroom the speed limit may be 10 mph. And in Ms. C's classes, the speed limit may be 133 mph. There are teachers and students who function effectively within each of these limits. Probably the major cause of teacher stress and eventual hostility is that the classroom is functioning beyond the teacher's personal limit, whether that limit be 10 mph or 133 mph. If a teacher wishes to have the students behave within her comfort range, then she cannot ignore any inappropriate behavior beyond her personal limit.

When teachers and administrators ignore inappropriate behavior in schools, they communicate clearly to the students that they may continue the inappropriate behavior. All schools have rules prohibiting certain behaviors. However, the "real rules" are those which are consistently enforced, not those which are ignored. Here are some examples of typical forbidden behaviors; however, on some campuses the behaviors violate the "official rules"—but not the "real rules".

Cussing on campus
Littering
Truancy and cutting classes
Walking around campus during class periods
Chewing gum or smoking
Being late to class
Showing up without appropriate work materials

School personnel who value specific rules, such as no cutting class or no chewing gum in class, for the most part obtain the desired results. Others, however, feel that they have no control over that particular behavior, ignore it, and hope that it will go away. But it never does. The point is that responsible adults are successful, regardless of the specific value, when they believe in the rule and take an active stance to stop the unacceptable behavior rather than ignore it.

## Encouraging Inappropriate Behavior

Teachers and parents sometimes encourage inappropriate behavior. Strange as it may seem, one often hears teachers and parents say, "I dare you to do that again", or "That was real cute. Why don't you save that and show it to your father when he gets home, so he can see what I've had to put up with all day?" Or "I'd like to see you do that again", or "Go for it; I'd like to see you try." Comments like these do not stop the behavior. Rather, they encourage the inappropriate behavior. To dare a junior-high or high-school youngster to repeat an inappropriate behavior—even when meant as sarcasm—is to invite compliance. Instead of telling the student directly to stop the behavior, the adult hopes that the student will interpret the comment as sarcasm and stop on his own. However, students in general and students with difficult discipline problems in specific do not respond positively to indirect communications. Unfortunately, when the student behaves as requested, the teacher or parent becomes even angrier at the student for showing poor judgment—by doing exactly what he has been told to do.

## Focusing on an Irrelevant Behavior

In this category of communication, the teacher focuses on a related behavior rather than on the real problem. This misdirection encourages the continuation of the inappropriate behavior.

The underlying structure of the following examples is basically the same in each case. The student is behaving inappropriately (Behavior A). The teacher does not tell him to stop the problem behavior (Behavior A). Instead, she demands that he do Behavior B, which she feels the student must do first before he stops Behavior A. In all the following examples, if the teacher focused on the real problem and stopped that problem (Behavior A), the demand for Behavior B would be irrelevant.

1. *Honesty about the Symptom.* The teacher demands that the student tell the truth about some inappropriate behavior, such as stealing, instead of demanding that he stop the behavior. She gets upset at the student for stealing and says, "Tell me the truth. No student of mine lies to me. Tell me what you did." The focus is on telling the truth rather than on stopping the stealing.

Some teachers and administrators put the student through a miniature Spanish Inquisition to get the truth, and they are usually successful. Yet they do not spend nearly as much time and energy trying to stop the inappropriate behavior as they do in getting at the truth. Certain youngsters are very straightforward and proudly tell about their latest misbehaviors. These youngsters have been programed over the years to be honest about their behaviors rather than to change them. The teacher has to ask herself whether she prefers that the student admit to his stealing (Behavior B) or stop stealing and never steal again (Behavior A). If the student stops stealing and never steals again, then he will have no reason to lie to his parents or his teacher. If the teacher demands that the student tell her the truth about his stealing, then she is encouraging him to do something inappropriate so that at some later date he will have something further to confess.

A similar situation occurs when a youngster either tears up his progress report ("report card", in some jurisdictions) or forges his parent's signature on it. The parents get upset at the school for not sending home the progress report by registered mail. If the parents demand that their child tell them the truth about the misbehavior, the counselor should ask them, "Would you prefer having your child maintain a good report card so he won't have to tear it up? Or would you prefer that he fail, tear up the report, but at least tell you the truth about it at some later date?" The parents need to see that if they get the child to act appropriately (getting a good report card—Behavior A), then his honesty about his misbehavior (Behavior B) is unnecessary and irrelevant.

*2. Concern about the Symptom.* The teacher demands that the student feel sorrow, guilt, remorse, or concern about the inappropriate behavior. She says, "Aren't you even sorry for what you did? I saw you do it with my own eyes, but when I asked you about it you lied to me. You don't even seem to care." The implication is that it is more important for the student to feel remorse, guilt, or sorrow than it is to change the inappropriate behavior.

The teacher should ask herself, "If he says that he is sorry, is it okay for him to do it again?" On every occasion the reply will be "No." If she doesn't want him to do it again, she must focus on the real problem and stop that problem instead of having the student feel sorry.

Some people, however, really feel that the student should feel sorry for his inappropriate behavior—but if the student does nothing inappropriate, then he will not have to feel sorry. No one brings children into the world to make them feel guilt, shame, and concern for things that they have never done. Yet parents and teachers often demand that students who are acting inappropriately feel sorry for their behavior. Remember that over the years students learn to act according to what adults demand or expect of them. Junior-high and high-school students often get away with inappropriate behavior by "feeling sorry" for it: "I said I'm sorry; what more do you want?"

The teacher needs to reply that she doesn't care if the student feels sorry or not. What is important is that he stop the inappropriate behavior and never do it again.

*3. Face the Problem.* In this situation the teacher says, "If you would just face up to the problem. . . ." This statement implies that facing the problem (whatever that might mean) is more important than eliminating the problem by changing the inappropriate behavior. Does she want him to face up to the problem and take responsibility for his actions, or does she want him to change the behavior? Often the youngster not only has to face up to the fact that he has a problem, but also he eventually will have to face up to the teacher, to the principal, to his parents, or even to the police. Wouldn't it be better for him just to change the behavior?

4. *Effort to Change.* In this communication pattern the teacher says, "Just make an effort." "Try to get to class on time." "Try to do your homework." "Just try to be nice for once in your life." Or "Just try to act like a human being instead of the animal that you are." These communications imply that it is more important to try to change than to actually change. Instead of telling the student to behave in a specific way, the teacher tells him to *try* to behave in that way. The implication is that the child is incapable of doing what is requested right now. The teacher needs to ask herself, "Is the student capable of doing what I have requested right now? If so, which would I like him to do right now—get to class on time, or try to get to class on time?"

It is interesting to note that adults use these statements on such relatively simple tasks as getting to class on time, taking out the garbage, and doing homework—even on high school students. Is the student really incapable of doing what is requested? If the student is capable, then he either behaves appropriately or he doesn't.

5. *Think about Your Behavior.* Under this category the teacher says, "Think before you act", or "Think twice before you do something stupid like that again." The implication is that the inappropriate behavior is okay as long as he thinks twice before he does it again. The question is, "Is it okay for him to continue to do what he is doing as long as he thinks it over and decides to pay the consequences?" Most adolescent crooks have thought it over quite a bit. In fact, the ones that get caught are generally those who haven't thought it over carefully enough. The question is, does the teacher want the student to continue stealing as long as he has thought it over, or does she want him to stop stealing?

One might imagine a student saying to a teacher, "I have thought it over. I have analyzed the advantages, the disadvantages, and the implications of my actions. I have decided that, at worst, you will get angry at me and possibly suspend me for a day or two. Taking full responsibility for my actions, I have decided to beat up John." One might have problems imagining a teacher replying, "I'm glad that you have thought it over; go right ahead and beat him up."

6. *Don't Get Caught.* Teachers and parents sometimes say, "Don't you ever let me catch you doing that again." The unspoken message is that it is okay to behave that way again just as long as you don't get caught. Ultimately, is it okay for the student to continue the inappropriate behavior as long as he is not caught, or should he stop the inappropriate behavior?

It appears that one of the nation's emerging codes of conduct is to do whatever you want: just don't get caught. This ethic is clearly reflected in movies, literature, television, in the way some people fill out tax forms, and in the behavior of some prominent role-models. But is this a value which teachers want to transmit to their students?

*7. Willingness to Discuss Reasons.* Some teachers and parents believe that in order to change inappropriate behavior the student should be encouraged to discuss the reasons for the behavior. The implication is that one cannot change inappropriate behavior without discussing the reasons behind the behavior. Does the adult want the youngster to talk to her about why he isn't going to school, or would she prefer to have him attend school? While it is important and highly recommended that communications improve, it is not recommended that the adult spend her time talking with the youngster about his negative and inappropriate behavior in an effort to get him to change. When she can get him to act appropriately, then she can spend her time talking with him about the positive aspects of life, rather than the negative ones. Adults should not spend their time talking to misbehaving students about their actions. Instead, they should get them to behave and then learn to communicate in a more meaningful way about positive things.

A mother complained that her 16-year-old daughter would not communicate. To illustrate that the daughter's communication was not necessarily the major problem, the counselor asked this question: "If your daughter went to a party, took drugs, stole from a liquor store, and came in after 3:00 a.m., and then told you all the details of her escapades, would you feel that the communication between you had improved?" Needless to say, improved communication about her daughter's inappropriate behavior was not what the mother really wanted. She really wanted to solve the problem of her daughter's inappropriate behavior, rather than her daughter's unwillingness to discuss her problems.

*8. Willingness to Learn and/or to Accept Help.* Some communication patterns are based on the notion that a student must be willing to learn or to accept help before he can learn. The following statements reflect this philosophy: "You have to be open to new experiences. You have to be self-motivated and willing to learn." "If you would just let me help you, I'm sure we could solve this problem." An excellent reflection of this philosophy would be the aphorism "You can lead a horse to water, but you can't make him drink."

Many educators subscribe to this belief, leading to a disastrous outcome for some students. They believe that they must motivate the student and get his willingness to learn before he will actually learn. While it is preferable that students be willing, it isn't reasonable to expect that they always will be. However, when it is imperative that the student learn what is required of him, one has to demand that he learn whether he is willing or not. Remember that although Helen Keller was far from willing to learn at first, her teacher expected and demanded that she do so. And she learned.

Intelligent junior-high or high-school students are often not self-motivated when they begin to learn a new subject, such as trigonometry or Latin. Moreover, most of them would not voluntarily take additional history or English courses. However, as they gain skills in the subject area, become more proficient at it, and see the relevance of the subject, many times they develop a fondness for the subject and pursue it further. Of course there is no guarantee that a student will learn to love any particular subject. After all, some people who read well choose not to read very much. A student who never learns to read, however, severely limits his choices in life. Learning gives students a choice.

The *Omnibus Personality Inventory* (Heist, 1968)*, a test measuring (in part) the intellectual orientation of college students, indicates that (on a national level) fewer than 10% of college students are intrinsically motivated to pursue ideas, abstractions, and learning purely for the sake of learning. One would expect the percentage of junior-high and high-school students so motivated to be even smaller. For that reason, it is important that teachers be prepared not only to encourage learning by making the process a positive one, but also that they be prepared to make the student do the work. If the warm, encouraging, positive approach fails, and the youngster has difficulty in learning to read or even in wanting to learn to read, it is the teacher's professional duty to do everything in her power to make the student learn to read and write whether he wants to or not. If at times it is necessary to force normal students to read, do their work, and be successful in school, then it is imperative that we also do this for special-education students or students who are failing. Research shows that one of the variables crucial to the learning process is the amount of time spent on task. Therefore, if a youngster is having difficulty, the teacher should use the best instructional skills and methodology available to increase the probability of successful learning, but more importantly she should have him spend more time on task.

*9. Learn from the Experience.* Teachers sometimes say, "Keep that up and you'll learn that crime doesn't pay." "I guess you'll have to learn from the School of Hard Knocks." "You'll have to learn that matches are dangerous and can burn you."

The hope is that students will learn from these negative experiences and gain insight into a universal truth that will keep them on the straight-and-narrow for the rest of their lives. However, prisons, burn wards, and cemeteries are full of people who didn't seem to learn. When a teacher

---

*Heist, Paul, and G. Young. *Omnibus Personality Inventory: Manual.* The Psychological Corporation, 1968.

communicates in this style, she implies that the student should keep up the inappropriate behavior, but learn from it. She needs to ask herself if she really wants the student to learn more subtle nuances about the behavior so that he becomes an expert at it, or if she wants him to stop the behavior.

In summary, the reader should remember that indirect communications do not focus on the real problem. If any responsible adult demands Behavior B, she will not be telling the student to stop Behavior A, and she will be setting the stage for the continuation of the inappropriate behavior. She must constantly ask herself, "What is the real problem here?" If she solves that problem (Behavior A), does she really need to concern herself with Behavior B?

### Abstract, Meaningless Directions

Instead of focusing on a competing, non-essential goal, some communications appear to focus on the real problem. However, they are so vague and abstract that they don't help to stop the inappropriate behavior. Consider the following meaningless directions: "Grow up." "If you respected me, you wouldn't do that." "You are not working up to your potential." "Act your age; be more responsible and mature."

This particular communication style is vague because it does not tell students specifically what to do. Furthermore, the directions have nothing to do with the inappropriate behavior in question, such as squirming, hitting, or spitting.

When the student gets out of his seat again, this is a clear message to the teacher that he has not grown up in the way that she would like. Instead of addressing the issue of whether or not he is grown up or mature, the teacher should tell him about sitting in his seat and not getting up until she tells him to do so.

In the same vein, when she says, "If you respected me, you wouldn't do that," she should tell herself, "If he does the behavior again, that is a clear message to me that he does not respect me; now, is there anything that I would like to tell him about getting out of his seat the next time he does it?"

It is necessary to define abstract terms such as "potential", "maturity", "love", and "common sense" in specific, concrete terms so that everyone knows exactly what is expected to occur. The teacher must ask herself, "What does the student need to do in specific, observable terms so that when he does it, I will think that he is working to his potential? Acting his age? Grown up? Responsible?"

One's operational definition of a student whom one likes and thinks is mature is a student who basically does what one thinks is right. If he doesn't act appropriately and doesn't do what one thinks is right, then generally one categorizes him as immature, irresponsible, and disagreeable. If teachers get the students to behave appropriately, they will like them better and generally categorize them as more mature, responsible, and as working to their potential.

Abstract, meaningless communications from parents and teachers can include such directions as "Go to school and have a nice day" or "Clean up the room." A student's interpretation may differ from the intended meaning. An acting-out youngster's definition of having a nice day at school may consist of showing up late, doing little work, and missing a few classes without getting caught. When talking to such a youngster, it is important to be specific and concrete: "Go to school, be there on time, stay there, and do your work."

The teacher's vague command to "Clean up the room" is a popular example; the student's definition of a clean room is much different from the teacher's. Many a youngster can live in an absolute pig-sty with things scattered everywhere and think that it is clean. If given this vague, abstract communication, once he has picked up a few things he is satisfied that the room is cleaned up. Some youngsters need to have the directions spelled out in specific and concrete terms: "Pick up all the paper from the floor and put it into the trash can; put your book and materials into the desk; and straighten all the rows of desks." Once the student is conditioned to these specific directions, the teacher can then generalize to the more abstract directions. However, if she gives abstract directions, and the student does not follow them, then she has a clear message from the student that her directives must be simple, clear, and more concrete.

On the whole, students think at a more concrete level than adults do. This thinking is readily apparent in a phone conversation with a young child. When asked if her mother is at home, the child says "Yes." After a short pause, it occurs to the caller to give the child the clearer directive "Go get your mother." Then the child hangs up and goes to get his mommy. While redialing, the caller formulates very specific and concrete directions: "Don't hang up the phone. Go get your mommy, and ask her to come to the phone now, please."

Most students outgrow the need for such very concrete thinking. Some youngsters, however—the loophole thinkers or junior lawyers—continue in this mode of behavior. These youngsters, who continually give teachers trouble in the classroom, need very specific and concrete directions initially. One can determine that this form of abstract communication works if the student does what is wanted. If he doesn't, then one needs to use a more specific, concrete, direct message.

## Statements of Fact

Another indirect communication pattern results when the teacher states the obvious, describing what the student is doing instead of giving a clear directive to stop the inappropriate behavior. For example: "You are acting out again." "You are not sitting in your seat today." "I see that you didn't bring your pencils and paper to class again."

This style of communication implies that although the teacher is observant, the student does not realize what he is doing and needs to be told.

Imagine a high-school teacher saying to a student, "I see that you didn't bring your books and paper to class." The student stops dead in his tracks with a puzzled look on his face and says, "No kidding. Gee, I thought I had them right here under my arm. I didn't even realize I didn't have them. I have a new form of learning-disability related to my tactile senses. I'm sure glad you told me. I'll go get my books right now." Of course, if this actually happened, the student would probably be suspended for insubordination.

A teacher tells a story that very succinctly illustrates the folly of this style of communication. A hyperactive fourth-grade boy was continually out of his seat and not doing his work. The teacher was in the corner of the room conducting a reading lesson when she observed him moving about the room. She said, "I see that you are out of your seat again." To which he replied, "No s____."

It is important to tell students specifically what to do, instead of just reiterating the obvious.

One of the best examples in this category of communications in the home is hearing the mother tell her child, "This is the biggest dump I have ever seen in my life." Try to decide what response would be reasonable from the child's perspective; perhaps: "Mom, you haven't lived very much. If you think this is a dump, you should see John's room. Maybe then you wouldn't pick on me."

**Classification Systems**

In this category of communication styles, the student is classified and labeled in a negative or derogatory fashion.

It is clear what power the labeling process has for either facilitating human potential or imprisoning it in a cage of limited expectations. Negative classifications are very common: "You are a bad boy." "You are a thief." "What a tomboy." "You're lazy." "Way to go, stupid." "You have an attitude problem." And so on.

Adults need to address specific behavior problems ("Get to school on time." "Do your homework." "Do these ten problems neatly and correctly in the next ten minutes." "Raise your hand before you speak."), instead of tagging the student with a negative label.

**Predictions**

Instead of giving clear directions to stop the behavior, teachers and parents sometimes tell the student what will become of him. They say, "You're going to spend your life in jail." "You'll never grow up." "You'll flunk out of school." "You won't amount to anything." Unfortunately, students—if told by significant adults over extended periods of time—seem to follow these self-fulfilling prophecies with amazing accuracy.

There was a very bright junior-high-school girl who was doing poorly in school. She spent more time talking about boys than doing her classwork, even though she was very capable. During a parent conference her mother said that it was not necessary for the girl to do well in school because she would be pregnant and drop out of high school just as all of her sisters had done. The mother was very accurate in her prediction; when the girl was a sophomore, she became pregnant and dropped out of school.

## Questions

This category has become one of our national pastimes. We have been so psychologized that almost everyone asks, "Why did you do that?" Here are other examples in this category: "What did I do to deserve a child like you?" "How long do you plan to continue misbehaving?" "How many times do I have to tell you?" "Were you born in a barn?" "Are you deaf? Didn't you just hear me say. . . ?"

Some youngsters become adept at coming up with reasonable answers to such questions. The teacher says, "How many times do I have to tell you?" The student responds, "Two thousand and thirty-three."

A mother says, "Were you born in a barn?" The child responds, "You should know; you were there."

If the student has a good enough reason for doing what he is doing, is it okay for him to continue the behavior? When teachers speak with the parents of failing students, the parents will invariably ask, "Why is Johnny flunking, and why does he hate school?" A teacher's response to such inquiries should be, "If he gives a good enough excuse why he hates school, then is it okay for him to never come again and continue to flunk?"

Actual interaction patterns show that a person gets exactly what she asks for. A teacher breaks up a student fight and typically asks, "Why are you fighting?" Both fighters reply, "He started it!" Then one says, "I did not; he called me a name." Then four other students join in at once to explain what "really" happened. By this time the teacher is confused and says, "Shut up! I don't want to hear about it. Both of you are coming with me to the principal's office."

Consider another scenario: When asked why they were fighting, the first student replies, "I was inappropriately toilet-trained, have weak ego-boundaries, and haven't found appropriate ways of displacing and venting my pent-up aggressions, hostilities, and frustrations." The second student responds, "I have deep-seated emotional problems, have always been extremely jealous of my older brother, and haven't learned to resolve this basic sibling rivalry. This fight is a projected attempt to resolve the conflict." The teacher then responds, "I'm sure glad that you told me why you're fighting. These seem to be very reasonable explanations, so please continue fighting and tell me when you have finished."

It is not really necessary to know the reasons for inappropriate behavior. If a teacher stops the behavior and the student never does it again, knowing why he behaved inappropriately is irrelevant. No one thinks to ask the better-behaved students in class why they never misbehave or even why they behave appropriately, so why would the teacher even consider asking acting-out students why? She should just get them to behave.

Being uninterested in the reasons for the child's misbehavior does not mean being insensitive to the child and his needs or what is going on in his world. Effective parents and teachers should all be as sensitive, caring, and knowledgeable as possible. However, understanding a child's needs is not an acceptable excuse for non-negotiable behaviors. Understanding a child's anger does not mean that adults can allow him to hurt or kill someone. The goal of educators is to teach children better ways to solve their problems, so that they are no longer problems. No parent asks a two-year-old child why he wets his pants; parents just continue training him until he learns to solve that problem and is successful. When he becomes successful, the reason why he wet his pants becomes irrelevant. An adult can be sensitive and caring in many areas and in many ways, but she doesn't need to know the reasons for inappropriate behavior. Teachers must be sensitive and reasonable, but they must also set the non-negotiable standards of expected behaviors and make the student perform the tasks successfully.

This culture psychologizes children and students by providing reasons for misbehavior. Parents and teachers have inadvertently created situations in which they actually tell the child the most popular reasons for his misbehavior. The child then uses those reasons as excuses for future inappropriate behavior.

A mother asks her four-year-old daughter why she punched her baby brother. The child says, "I don't know." The mother helps out with a variety of popular theories: "Is it just because you're angry and upset?" "Is it jealousy?" "Frustration?" "Are you tired and need to go to bed?" The child later parrots these and similar excuses in an attempt to get out of trouble. The ultimate question is: Even if she is tired, frustrated, angry, or jealous, is it still okay for her to hit her baby brother?

The following example illustrates how we psychologize and give our children and students excuses for their inappropriate behavior. In a counseling session a mother asked her boy, who was tapping his fingers and squirming around in his chair in a very loud and obnoxious way, "Do you have to go to the bathroom?" This question was apparently an attempt to stop his inappropriate behavior. The boy, not understanding his mother's cue, didn't verbally respond but continued to act inappropriately. After the mother made a few more vague and indirect attempts to stop the inappropriate behavior, she finally said in exasperation, "Look, I mean it—if you have to go to the bathroom, tell me." The boy was a fast learner on the second cueing and replied, "I have to go to the bathroom."

For the inherently curious, here are three of the most common reasons "why" children act inappropriately: (1) They are just like adults and therefore procrastinate. They will put off what they don't like doing and will do everything else first. (2) They want to find out where they belong, who is in control, and whether or not they can count on the significant adult for leadership, guidance, and parenting. (3) They have learned that they can get away with it.

There are no new reasons why students choose not to attend school, just the old excuses: "It is boring." "We always learn the same stupid stuff." "I don't like it." "The teachers are dumb." "They are there just for their paychecks." "It's a waste of time; I'd rather get a job to pay for a car." Will any of these excuses make a difference if the student drops out of school? If he doesn't learn to read and write? If he doesn't get a high school diploma? If he can't maintain a job? If he ends up on welfare? It is hoped that no teacher will accept any excuse for illiteracy and will take an active, assertive stance to insure that the student completes his work and learns the necessary academic skills.

### Behavior Modification Contracts, Threats, or If/Then Contracts

We sometimes communicate to the student that he has a choice of whether or not to behave. We communicate this idea with If/Then Contracts: "If you do these ten problems, then you'll get. . . ."; "If you do that one more time, I'll. . . ."; "Don't ever do that again, or else. . . .".

Behavior Modification specialists have used this technique successfully in stopping inappropriate behaviors and extensively shaping many appropriate behaviors. They have developed a rather sophisticated terminology and methodology for implementing the process of changing inappropriate behavior. "Grandma's Law" provides a simplistic way of stating the complexities of Behavior Modification: "If you eat your peas, you get dessert. If you don't eat your peas, you will be spanked and sent to bed." (If X, then Y; if not X, then Z.) This approach works for young children, sales people on incentive systems, piece-workers, anyone who buys into and/or is willing to go along with the Behavior Modification program, and dogs. For someone who does not fit into one of those categories and is in direct conflict with the teacher's intentions, this approach seldom works.

One of the unforeseen consequences of these statements and contracts is that the student learns quickly that he can refuse to do what is requested unless there is something in it for him or the "or else" is sufficiently negative to curtail his behavior. If we use Behavior Modification terms, we inadvertently help to set up contingencies of reinforcement that encourage selfish, greedy, "me first" behaviors. Now when teachers tell students to stop a particular act, many of the students respond with, "Or else what? What will you give me?" Or in some situations when the student does not care about the particular reward offered, he will say, "Go ahead; suspend me. I don't care."

In the same vein, some parents offer their underachieving but capable children money to get better grades. They still don't improve their grades—either because they don't want to or because the money isn't enough. One student was making more money not going to school and selling drugs than was offered by his parents to go to school and get good grades.

Analyzing these if/then contracts from a communications-system perspective, the teacher will find that she has clearly stated that the student's behavior is his choice. He may choose to do X or not, depending on whether or not he is willing to suffer the consequences. Many students who are difficult discipline problems are more than willing to accept the consequences. Many students, when given the choice of acting correctly, or staying in from recess, or staying after school, or writing 100 sentences, or being suspended, will choose to take the consequences rather than behave appropriately. Under these circumstances, the teacher must ask herself whether she really wants the student to have the option. Is either choice all right with her? Does she want him to make the choice which leads to punishment, or does she want to take an assertive stance to prevent inappropriate behavior and ensure his success?

Some parents and teachers argue the importance of letting a child or student make his own choices and accept responsibility for his own behavior. This is an admirable objective; however, it should be qualified. One qualification is to limit his decisions initially to those that are non-critical to his long-range well-being—the clothes that he wears, the foods that he eats (given a wide choice of healthy foods), or the homework that he does first. Generally, these are decisions that are not life- or health-threatening and that do not go against the family's values. Another qualification is to allow the student or child the freedom to make decisions in the critical areas only when he has demonstrated success in decision-making. A long history of poor decision-making is a clear indication that the student or child needs assistance in making more appropriate decisions.

For example, if a child chooses to eat ice cream and huge amounts of sugar and does not choose to brush his teeth, is the parent willing to allow him to accept the consequences? If a high-school student decides not to go to school, indicating that he is willing to accept the consequences of flunking out, is the parent willing to allow him that option? Is the parent willing to allow her sixteen-year-old daughter to become a heroin addict and to support that habit by being a prostitute?

Students and children should be allowed to make as many decisions as they are capable of making within a wide range of acceptable choices. However, they should not be allowed to make decisions when they have consistently made poor decisions or when one of the alternatives is detrimental to their health or well-being. When the student acts appropriately and demonstrates good judgment, the responsible adult can give him more freedom, let him make more decisions, and trust him.

If parents indicate to a counselor that their seventeen-year-old son is old enough to make his own decisions, the counselor would say, "Fine; let him make his own decision and flunk out of school. But don't get angry with him, be hostile, or belittle him for making such a decision. If you are willing to let him make that decision, then praise him for being willing to be responsible for the consequences of his actions. If, however, you take this position, then let him pay the consequences and don't constantly bail him out when he gets into trouble." (Parents often say that they want their child to pay the consequences, yet they continually save him from those consequences. In so doing, they not only teach the child that he doesn't have to make good decisions, but they also teach him that he doesn't have to pay the price for poor decisions. The child also learns that he cannot count on his parents for reliable guidance.)

The teacher who says to a student "You may do these ten problems now, or you may stay after school and do them", should ask herself "Would I really like the student to put off doing his work and stay after school to complete it?" and "If the student chooses not to do the problems and to stay after school, is it likely that he will act appropriately for the rest of the day and not disrupt the educational process for any other student?"

Probably, the answer to both of these questions is "No." Perhaps, then, the teacher should just tell the student, clearly and specifically, "John, do these ten problems, neatly and correctly, within the next fifteen minutes," instead of giving him a chance to make a choice which will create unnecessary complications for both of them. After all, why should the teacher punish herself by staying after school?

Many teachers, however, believe that even when they give a problem student this clear direction, he will not comply. That is why they rarely use this straightforward approach. However, when you analyze how teachers enforce if-X-then-Y contracts, you will see how illogical and inconsistent this belief is. Teachers who believe in if/then contracts will not give clear directives in trying to make the student do his ten problems (the X part of the contract), but they will illogically and inconsistently turn right around and give very clear directives to make him do the consequences (the Y part of the contract). Most teachers by giving clear directions are very successful at making a student do the Y portion of the contract but still believe that they can't give clear directions to the student on the X portion of the contract because he will not follow them. To get out of this particular predicament, teachers must do either one or another of the following: (1) analyze why they believe the student to be incapable (review Chapter II); (2) give clear directions on the X portion of the contract and see what happens; or, if the clear message does not seem to work, (3) develop back-up techniques to make sure that the student will follow directions. (This latter contingency will be discussed in Chapters V and VI.)

Some teachers, because of their beliefs, still feel that the student should be given a choice. Any teacher who considers an if-X-then-Y contract necessary should consider a choice like this one: "John, you may have the choice of doing these ten problems now, or staying after school. However, if you choose to stay after school to do the problems, then you will sit in your seat with your mouth shut, you will not talk to, disrupt, or disturb any other student in this classroom, and you will do twenty problems instead of ten as well as any other work that you have missed. Now, which would you like to choose to do?"

Teachers are paid to educate students, not to have them sit around and do nothing. If the student chooses not to learn, the teacher has certain professional obligations:

(1) Prevent that student from disrupting the educational opportunities and learning processes of other students;

(2) Do everything possible to make him learn whether he wants to or not; and

(3) Notify the parents, and get a clear understanding of what they want done in regard to this situation.

Here is one last observation on Behavior Modification and If/Then Contracts. Teachers who successfully employ behavior modification in their classrooms often use a time-out screen as a way either to prevent reinforcing the student's inappropriate behavior or to withdraw from the student the rewards of a positive classroom environment. When the student emerges from behind the screen, the teacher selectively reinforces successive approximations of appropriate behavior. This technique, if done properly, is usually highly successful.

The obvious question to ask teachers who successfully use this program is how they initially get the student to go behind the time-out screen. One teacher's response was, "Well, that is part of the program. He has to go; he has no choice. I just tell him to go behind the screen for ten minutes."

"Does the student want to go behind the screen on his own? Does he like going behind the screen?"

"No."

"You mean that he is not self-motivated to go behind the screen?"

"That's correct."

"What do you do if a student initially gives you trouble about going behind the screen?"

"I tell him to go behind the screen, now. If he doesn't, I put him behind the screen."

"Does the student stay behind the screen when you put him there? If he doesn't, what do you do?"

"I tell him to stick his head back behind that screen and not to come out until I tell him to."

It is interesting to note what happens when this teacher gives clear and specific directions: she is successful at getting students to go to the time-out screen and to stay there until they are told to come out. Yet when she wants a student to do ten math problems, she doesn't give the same clear message. Instead, she gives the student a choice of doing the problems or going behind the time-out screen.

If the teacher really believes that the behavior modification technique causes the student's behavior to improve, why doesn't she set up a behavior modification program to shape successive approximations, using appropriate reinforcement schedules, to get the student behind the time-out screen in the first place? Teachers usually indicate that that procedure would be a waste of time and that students have to go behind the time-out screen because it is a part of the school program. One might argue that the time-out screen is a waste of time and the completion of the schoolwork should be made a required part of "the program".

The teacher should tell the difficult student exactly what she wants him to do and make him do it, rather than give him the choice of doing it or not. If he doesn't do what she tells him to do, then she must develop effective back-up techniques to make him do the goal behavior. (See Chapters V and VI.)

## Punishments

Punishment is actually a sub-category of the behavior modification if/then contract. (If you do not do X, then I will punish you with Y.) These elements have been separated because there are some special observations that need to be made about how successful parents and teachers are at punishing children—even though the punishment usually does not accomplish the desired goals that the adults wished for. When parents or teachers punish the child, they are very successful at getting the child to submit to the punishment, even though the child did not want to submit. Yet this successful act of punishing the child usually does not stop the inappropriate behavior.

How can parents and teachers be successful in one area of the child's behavior (punishing him) and at the same time be unsuccessful in another area (getting him to do his schoolwork)? The teacher who couldn't get the student to do the ten problems, but could get the student to go behind the time-out screen, is a prime example. A comparison of both messages will make clear that the teacher got the behavior that she requested.

In the first instance, she said, "If you don't do the ten problems, I will punish you by sending you to time-out. Either choice is okay with me." (Behavior-modification people would not see time-out as a punishment. It is strictly a way of removing the student and preventing his being reinforced for negative behavior or a way of removing him from the rewards of a positive classroom environment.) In the second instance, when she was successful at getting the student to go behind the screen, she told him specifically and clearly, "Go to time-out right now, and I mean it." She gave the student no choice—and he did what he was told to do.

In the school environment, teachers repeatedly say, "If you don't stop that right now, you will be in detention this afternoon." The punishment may vary, but the student is always given the choice of doing the work or taking the punishment. In most instances, the difficult student elects to take the punishment. It is amazing that the teacher can get the student to do the punishment, whether it is writing 100 sentences, going to detention, or going to the principal's office, but she can't get the student to do the original task. In the home situation, parents who can't get their child to do his homework are very successful at keeping the child on restriction for a month.

They can successfully send him to his room, but they cannot stop him from throwing a temper-tantrum. When parents or teachers are unsuccessful, they usually use a variation of the "if/then" contract. When they are successful, no matter what the particular behavior is, they usually give very clear messages to the child and no choice in the matter.

A mother tells of an instance when she was angry at her son because he was sarcastically teasing her one day. She began to chase him with a broom, becoming increasingly frustrated when she couldn't catch him. She finally shouted to him, "Stand still so I can hit you!" He obeyed, and she hit him.

Another example involves a divorced mother who had come into counseling with her two sons, aged 9 and 15. Her older son was giving her a lot of trouble, flunking school, and ditching. She had no control over him and couldn't get him to do anything that she wanted him to do. The methods which she had tried to get her son to go to school and to improve his grades were explored. She said that she had tried everything, and she proceeded to list the methods which she had tried. The latest method that she had tried was spanking. One might assume that she had spanked him when he was much younger, but she said that the incident had happened the previous week. Since the fifteen-year-old towered over her, she was asked to tell exactly what she did and said to him when she spanked him. (Remember, this mother's initial complaint was that she had no control over her son and couldn't get him to do anything.)

She said, "I was so mad at him for punching his little brother in the mouth that I told him to go to his room and think about what he had done, and in five minutes I was going to come up to his room and spank him."

"Did he go to his room and stay there for five minutes?"

"You're damned right! I was so mad at him, I could have killed him."

"What happened after the five minutes were up?"

"I went upstairs, walked into his room, and demanded that he stand up, take off his own belt, and hand it to me. After he had done that, I told him to bend over the bed, and I hit him with the belt ten times."

"Do you think that your son wanted to be spanked?"

"No."

The counselor pointed out that she had been very successful at getting her son to do what she wanted even when he didn't want to. She had got him to go to his room, take off his belt, bend over, and take a spanking. When she was very clear and direct in her communications, he followed them. But she was using vague and indirect communications concerning his school problems. She lectured him and tried a variety of "if/then" contracts. He could do his work—or become a bum. If he didn't go to school, he wouldn't be able to hold down a job in later life. If he kept acting like that, he would end up just like his dad.

Even parents who are child-abusers are usually very successful at punishing their children, even though they haven't been successful at getting them to do what they want them to do in other areas. Certainly no one advocates child abuse. Yet it is apparent that adults are successful at punishing children in the most amazing ways. The principles which underlie their success can and should be used in more positive ways. The use of clear and specific directions to get the child to behave appropriately works. There is no need to rely on physical punishment.

### Wishes, Wants, and Shoulds

In this category, adults say such things as "I wish you wouldn't do that." "I want you to stop hitting John." "You should know better." The adult states a preference, but does not give a clear statement of what she expects the child to do.

Consider the following example: A teacher says to a student, "I wish you wouldn't do that. You know how upset and angry it makes me." A difficult student might reply, "Well, that's your problem. Why don't you change? Then maybe you'll get off my back."

The mother of a student said to him, "I want you to do the dishes."

Her son replied, "So what? I want a million dollars."

With that he walked out the door and was gone for three days, a clear indication that the "I want" message was perceived as a preference and not as a demand.

In one "Dennis the Menace" cartoon Dennis's mother drags him into his messy room. A defiant Dennis says, "Why should I clean up my room? *You're* the one who wants it clean!" The cartoon points out a truth: both parties must want the same results in order for the "I want" statement to be successful. When there is a confrontation of wills, the adult must be more specific, concrete, and assertive in order to get results.

Parents of older children often say, "He is sixteen years old and he should know better."

He *should* know better, but he has clearly demonstrated that he is unwilling to change his behavior. If his behavior is a problem to the parents, are they willing to change it, even though the child isn't co-operative? When there is clearly a confrontation of wills, the parents should not communicate in wishes, wants, shoulds, preferences, or hopes. They should instead communicate in direct, specific terms what they expect him to do. If he does not respond, then they should make him do it. (This procedure will be discussed in Chapters V and VI.)

### Reasoning, Inspiring, Explaining, and Lecturing

Sometimes an adult doesn't really believe that the student understands the implications of his actions. Therefore, she tries to teach him and explain to him, over and over and over again, the implications of his behavior. Whenever an adult begins one of many pat, singsong lectures, the student already knows what she is going to say. Chances are that he's heard it a thousand times before and could easily repeat the speech verbatim. The implications of this communication pattern are insulting to the student: Is the student stupid? Does he really fail to understand the simple cause-and-effect relationship which the adult is trying to teach him? (If you don't do your homework, you will fail the class. If you don't go to school, you will fail school. If you keep stealing, you will go to jail.) It is counterproductive to waste any more time talking, lecturing, or explaining to the student what he needs to do, because he already understands what is expected of him. The teacher needs to spend her time and energy in developing strategies to insure that he does what she wants him to do, rather than in developing better lectures to convince him.

### Non-verbal Comments

Non-verbal messages need to agree with verbal messages. For example, when a student acts inappropriately, the teacher cannot smile or laugh as she tells him to stop the behavior. When she gives the student a clear verbal message to stop the behavior, she also needs to add congruent, non-verbal components, such as tone of voice, body posture, and distance. In so doing, she conveys to the student that she really means what she says.

Sometimes, indirect non-verbal messages communicate to the student that the teacher doesn't expect him to behave and that she sees him as incapable of behaving. For example, she segregates the student from other students because he can't control himself, she watches him more closely because she doesn't trust him, or she locks up certain things because he might be tempted by them. She thus communicates to the student that she doesn't expect him to behave. Inadvertently, she is encouraging him to continue acting inappropriately.

Separating a student from others or allowing him to work at his own pace fosters and encourages the student's (and sometimes the parents') belief that he is incapable of learning in a regular classroom. This is not to say that there is no place for special education or individualized instruction; legitimate cases and situations do require such intervention. However, few claims that a student is incapable of functioning effectively in a regular classroom are substantiated by observable facts. If teachers and parents focused on the real problem and developed intervention strategies to ensure the student's success within the regular classroom, then they wouldn't need to separate the student or have him work at his own pace so much.

## Summary

Although all the communication patterns discussed here occasionally work with some students, they do not always work with hard-to-handle students. Because these communication patterns rely on vague, indirect, unclear messages, the adult who uses them fails to tell the student to correct or to stop the inappropriate behavior. Communication-system theory states that what people say is a reflection of what they mean. These vague, indirect communications, then, reflect an underlying belief-system that the parent and/or the teacher does not see the student as being capable of doing what is requested. For example, the statement "Try to sit still" does not tell the student to sit still but, rather, reflects the adult belief-system that the student is incapable of doing what is requested. There are multitudes of beliefs (or excuses) for not making the student sit still.

The faulty belief-systems lead to vague and indirect communication patterns that are generally ineffective. To be effective in dealing with children, teachers and parents need to use specific and direct messages. The next chapter discusses in greater detail how some parents and teachers use direct, effective communications to stop inappropriate behavior.

# Chapter IV: Effective Communication Patterns

In the past two chapters, we covered the two major elements of this model—(1) analysis of erroneous parent and teacher belief-systems and (2) analysis of ineffective communication and interaction patterns. In this chapter we shall explore effective communication patterns that stop inappropriate behavior, and we shall contrast these with ineffective communication patterns.

To stop inappropriate behavior, the teacher must decide on the goal behavior and tell the student—in very specific, clear, and concrete terms— exactly what she wants him to do, when she wants him to do it, and to what degree of accuracy she wants the task completed. When she gives clear and direct messages, she conveys specifically what is to be done, and she also reflects an underlying belief-system which states: (1) It is reasonable to expect and to tell the student to do the particular behavior; (2) The student is capable of doing what is asked; and (3) The student must do what is requested. This position is not authoritarian, hostile, dogmatic, or arbitrary. It is used for non-negotiable, well-thought-out, valued behaviors and rules that affect the student's well-being—along with the well-being of other class members and of the teacher as well.

Given children's concrete understanding-level of reality, it becomes clear that to stop inappropriate behavior teachers have to break the goal behavior into small, behaviorally concrete parts and must specifically tell the student to stop the inappropriate behavior. For example, if a teacher says, "John, sit in your seat," and John sits in his seat but then gets up right away, she will have to add, "John, sit in your seat *right now,* and stay there until I tell you to get up." If John sits in his seat and stays there, but does no work and disrupts the class, then she will have to close the loopholes by saying, "John, sit in your seat now. Stay there until I tell you to get up. While you are there, do these ten problems neatly and correctly within the next fifteen minutes. Do not talk to anyone; keep your hands and feet to yourself."

She will know how concrete and specific she needs to be by observing what the student does. If the student is not doing what she wants him to do, that is a clear indication that he hasn't gotten the message. She must make the message clearer and more specific. She will know—not only by observing the student's behavior, but also by what he tells her—whether or not she needs to be more specific. For example, she thinks that she is giving the student a clear message, but the student doesn't do exactly what she wants him to do. When confronted, he says, "I'm doing exactly what you said." Then she knows that she must be more specific.

Telling the student what to do will not always produce the desired behavior. Sometimes the teacher must tell the student and also back up the instruction behaviorally (back-up techniques will be discussed in the next chapter). However, in most situations, just telling the student what to do clearly and directly does work.

When parents are questioned about how they get their children to behave in specific situations, they reveal their own use of clear directives:

When you got your son to make his bed on the tenth request, how did you get him to do it? Usual answer: "I told him to make his bed right now."

When you were successful at keeping your daughter on restriction, how did you do that? Usual answer: "I told her that she was on restriction and she was not to see anyone, talk to anyone on the phone, or watch TV."

When your son threw a temper-tantrum and you couldn't take it anymore, what did you do? Usual answer: "I sent him to his room." How did you do that? Answer: "I told him to go to his room immediately, and I meant it."

When teachers are questioned about how they get their "problem" students to do as they are requested, the teachers also reveal that they rely on clear directives:

When you sent this uncontrollable student to the principal's office, how did you do it? Usual answer: "I gave him a referral card and told him to go to the principal's office."

When you made the student write 100 sentences, how did you do that? Usual answer: "He had no choice. I told him to write the sentences and have them here by tomorrow."

When you placed the student on after-school detention, how did you get him to stay? Usual answer: "I told him that he had detention and he had to be there." If he did not show up, what do you do? Usual answer: "I call the parents and let them know that he has detention. The next day I have his last-period teacher hold him in class. I go get him, and he serves his detention. Students know, and they quickly learn that when I say they have detention, they serve it."

Teachers are often successful at getting students to do amazing things—all of which the students did not want to do. Yet some of these teachers feel that they have no control or influence over these students. Teachers who feel that they have "no control" sometimes have students stand on a line during recess; put their nose in a circle on the blackboard for over fifteen minutes; stay after school; come to school on Saturdays to make up missed school days; or bend over and get four swats.

These teachers seem to have difficulty in getting students to do what they want only when they use vague, indirect communications on the initial interaction, because two minutes later they will give a clear directive, usually punishing the student in some way, and then the student will do as they requested.

Consider a junior-high-school music-teacher telling her rambunctious choir, "When you are standing still, we shall sit down." (Implication: When all of you are standing still, then we *will* sit down; until that time, I'll wait for you to choose to want to stand still.) About a minute later, at the top of her voice, she says, "You didn't hear me. . . ." (Implication: These students have impaired hearing.) "I said, when you're standing still, we shall sit down." Some minutes later under the teacher's angry stare, the students finally stood still. Then she said, "Fine. All of you sit down now." They all sat down immediately. The teacher used two different communication patterns within a few minutes with two different outcomes, and surely the teacher felt that she had no control over the students.

Remember the earlier example of the mother who couldn't get her fifteen-year-old son to go to school and stay there, but who was successful at spanking him? A first-grade teacher provided a similar school-related example. She talked about a student who wouldn't do anything that she wanted him to do. When asked what he did and what she had tried in order to prevent him from misbehaving, she said that every time she gave directions, he whistled. At first she ignored the behavior, hoping that it would go away. She then tried several tactics: "Good little boys don't do that when I am giving instructions."; "If you keep that up, you will have to stay in during recess."; and "Now, class, let's all turn and look at John, and when he is finished whistling, we shall begin." None of her approaches worked.

"What did you do when you had had all you could take and got really angry at him?"

"Well, I wasn't feeling too well, and he was really bugging me. Finally, I just said, 'Stand up right this minute, clean off your desk, put your chair in, go outside, stand on this side of the door where I can see you, and whistle until you get tired of whistling. Then you may come back into this classroom.' "

"Did he do all the things that you told him to do?"

"Yes. He stood out there and whistled for over fifteen minutes. The only problem was that he was up to his old whistling tricks again after a few hours."

At this juncture, it was pointed out to her that she had been successful at getting him to do exactly what she had told him to do—go outside and whistle. Yet, in attempting to stop the classroom whistling, she had never told him directly and emphatically, "Stop whistling, and never whistle again in this classroom."

When issuing clear directives, teachers do need to exercise discretion, however. A male teacher once held in three acting-out sixth-grade boys during recess. One of the youngsters indicated that he had to go to the bathroom.

The teacher said, "Tough; you have to wait."

The teacher was called away and left the three boys unsupervised in his room. As he was leaving, the one boy, bouncing up and down, indicated that he *really* had to go to the bathroom.

The teacher then said sarcastically, "If you have to go, do it in the trash can."

When the teacher returned in a few minutes, he found that the student who could not wait had followed his directions exactly. When the teacher confronted the student with his actions, one of the other students said, "Well, he did just what you said."

Even in complicated situations, teachers are successful when they give clear directives. One teacher described her problems with a particular third-grade student. He refused to do his classwork and was very argumentative; if she said that something was black, he insisted that it was white. She felt that she was unable to control him and that her efforts to discipline him were further handicapped by the fact that his parents seemed to support the student's inappropriate behavior. This support was indicated by the mother's comments to the teacher (given in front of the principal): "You don't really have the personality to be able to teach my child." "I don't want my child to become a robot and do what everyone else is doing." "I'm the only one who understands him and can really get him to do his work." The mother suggested to both the teacher and the principal that the student be put in a corner for two or three days and not be allowed to work. According to the mother, this action would motivate the student because of his competitive nature. Because he would want to keep up with his peers, he would happily go back to work.

Reluctantly, the school staff agreed to try the mother's approach. The teacher kept the student in a corner of the room for over seven days, but he never wanted to do his work. The teacher finally relayed this fact to the mother. The news surprised her because she was sure that he would choose to do the work on his own.

In spite of parental interference, this teacher had handled for seven days an acting-out, argumentative student who must have been bored out of his mind.

When asked what the student did during those seven days, the teacher said that he did absolutely nothing. On further inquiry, she said, "He tried to act up on a couple of occasions, but I told him to sit there and keep his mouth shut until he was ready to do his work like the rest of the students in the class. Then, and only then, could he move back to his regular seat and be a part of the class."

It's surprising that she believed she could not control the student or make him do his work even after she had so successfully kept him in a corner, doing absolutely nothing, for seven days. The teacher's power to stop inappropriate behavior was even more remarkable, given the fact that the parents were actively supporting the student's inappropriate behavior and had sabotaged her efforts to control him.

Parents and teachers are successful at punishing students by using direct communications even though the punishment does not solve the problem and in many cases may actually cause other problems. At a school P.T.A. meeting, some parents told of the trouble they had with their son's telling lies. In an effort to stop the child from lying they created a public liar's porch. Whenever they caught their son in a lie, they made him stand out on the liar's porch for hours so that everyone in the community would know that he had lied. Supposedly, this shaming technique worked so effectively that other parents in the community started using the same method. Then they extended the technique to publicly punish one child who was a bed-wetter. They made the six-year-old child put on a diaper and stand on the porch for hours on end. These people did not stop to address the real problems, yet they were successful at getting their children to stay out on the porch for some time. When asked if the children liked doing this "porch duty" and, if not, how they got the children to stay out on the porch without running away, they replied that they just told them that they had to do it whether they liked it or not.

All of these examples illustrate one major point: When an adult gives clear, direct communications to a child, and the child has no choice but to comply, the adult will be very successful at getting him to do just about anything. Remember, some adults are "successful" in spite of the fact that they focus on the wrong issue. One "good" spanking, public shaming, or other punishment technique works with some youngsters, especially with easy-to-raise, compliant children. However, generally speaking, focusing on the wrong issue and then doling out punishment rarely solves the real problem; this process only serves to reinforce the adult's belief that he or she has no control over the child.

When adults use different techniques, methods, and approaches, they convey different underlying belief-systems. When *successful,* an adult communicates two basic beliefs: (1) the belief that it is reasonable for her to take over and be in an authoritative position, and (2) the belief that the student is capable of doing what is requested of him. In addition, the adult communicates these beliefs to the student in specific, clear, direct, and concrete terms; she gives the student no choice; and if need be she backs up the demand in order to convey to the student that he must do what was requested. (The last point will be discussed in Chapter V.)

When an adult is *unsuccessful,* she communicates the opposite beliefs: (1) the belief that she does not have the ability or that it is not her right, responsibility, or duty to change the behavior, and (2) the belief that the student is incapable of doing what is requested. Because of these beliefs, she communicates to the student in vague, abstract, indirect communication patterns; she gives the student a choice of whether or not to comply with her directives; and she backs up her abstract, indirect communications with punishment that is not successful in stopping the behavior and which conveys to the student that he can keep doing the inappropriate behavior as long as he is willing to accept the punishment.

Even with an understanding of the principles of communications theory, some people feel uncomfortable in implementing the successful techniques. They may feel that this method smacks of authoritarianism. In some cases, it also reminds them of their own parents' behaviors which they disliked when they were children.

This is not, however, an authoritarian position; rather, it is an authoritative, assertive position, which is used only in absolutely non-negotiable behaviors. Communication is not hostile, aggressive, or angry; rather, it is loving and caring. The goal is not to make robots out of students. The real goal is to make them successful, skilled, independent people who use good judgment and make appropriate, life-enhancing decisions.

Many teachers and parents say that they are successful on the tenth attempt only because they are furious at the student and are ready to kill him. Actually, the hostility and anger are not what determine success. Rather, it is the fact that they finally mean what they say, and that they say it clearly and specifically. Parents and teachers can be equally successful at getting the student to obey the first time he is told if they initially say the same thing that they say on the tenth time, but without the hostility and aggression.

As an example, visualize this scenario: The mother comes home from a hard day at work. She enters the house and sees that the garbage has not been emptied.

(Step 1) She walks over to her adolescent son, who is stretched out on the couch watching TV, and says, "Didn't I tell you to take out the garbage this morning before school?" Implication: I'm not telling you to take the garbage out right now; I'm just questioning my own sanity and memory and wondering if, in fact, I did tell you to take out the garbage this morning.

(Step 2) The son still does not take out the garbage. The mother asks, "Will you please take out the garbage?" Implication: I'm not telling you to take it out; I'm just asking you if you are willing to do so.

(Step 3) The son at this point responds with either of the following answers. The first is, "Yes, I will take it out." (Meaning: Yes, I will take it out, but it will be sometime between now and the time I die.) The second and probably more popular response is, "Yes, just as soon as this program is over."

The mother continues her chores, preparing dinner and wishing that once in a while someone would take care of her needs. One hour later, she walks back into the room where her son is still watching TV, and the garbage is still where it was.

(Step 4) She blows up, and says, "Why don't you do what I ask you to?" Implication: I just want to know some good reasons.

(Step 5) "How many times do I have to tell you before you do what I ask?" Implication: I want to know how many more times I will have to ask before you will comply.

(Step 6) "You know this makes me madder than hell at you when you act this way." Implication: I'm just telling you how I feel at this point.

(Step 7) "You know that we all have jobs around here, and if everyone did his job it would make things a lot easier on me, and it would be a much nicer place to live." Implication: This is a statement of fact—we all have jobs, and, yes, it would be nicer if everyone did his job. This is Long Lecture Number Three, which her son could probably repeat verbatim.

(Step 8) "If you don't start growing up and taking more responsibility around this house, you will be on restriction for the rest of your life." Implication: Abstract, meaningless terms, coupled with an "if/then" contract.

(Step 9) And so on and so on, until the mother cannot take it any longer.

(Step 10) Mom has had it. At this point, she walks over, turns off the TV, walks over to her son, gets eye to eye with him, and says, "TAKE OUT THE GARBAGE, RIGHT NOW." If he doesn't comply immediately, she says, "LET ME HELP YOU GET STARTED THIS VERY SECOND." She takes him by the arm and moves him toward the garbage. At this stage the son says, "Okay, okay, Mom; I'll take out the garbage. Don't get hysterical."

Some mothers say that the only way they can get their children to do what they want is to get angry, to be upset, and to scream. However, if they say on the first time—cutting out Steps 1 through 9—what they finally say on the tenth time, they can achieve the same results with less stress on everyone.

Here is the same scenario with more effective patterns of communication. The mother comes home and sees that the garbage has not been taken out. She walks in, turns off the TV, gets eye to eye with her son, and calmly but firmly says, "Take out the garbage right now." Again, if he doesn't comply immediately, she says, "Let me help you get started immediately, and, from now on, when I tell you to takc out the garbage, do it when I ask you the first time." As her son is taking out the garbage, he can be overheard saying, "But, Mom, you don't understand; I have at least nine more steps before you mean it."

After the mother has used this method several times, the son will get the message that she means what she says on the first time instead of on the tenth, and he will develop the habit of complying without constant reminders. It is not necessarily the hostility and the anger that make the child comply. Rather, it is the clear communication and commitment to meaning what is said that works. An important secondary side-effect of this method is that it takes away the impetus to argue. Now the mother no longer engages in ten to fifteen nagging attempts to get her son to do something; the repetition that tends to make them both angry is no longer present.

Sometimes the issue of controlling the student comes up, and some people object to trying to tell the student what, where, when, or how to do everything. Such complete control is neither the goal, the desire, the intent, nor the outcome of this approach. This model is not a comprehensive child-rearing nor classroom-management method. It is simply a way of getting children and students to do what is wanted of them when it is imperative that they do so.

Children's behaviors can be divided into three categories: "non-negotiable", "preferred", and "who cares?". The student has the freedom to make his own choices and decisions about those behaviors that are "preferred" and "who cares?" and to pay the consequences of his actions within reasonable limits. Only in the category of "non-negotiable" behaviors does the teacher or parent implement a method in which the student initially has no choice until he learns how to do this behavior consistently on his own.

People get locked into arguing over who is going to make the "final choices and value judgments" that are in the best interests of the student in this "non-negotiable" category. But arguing over philosophical concerns about the ultimate, universal truth or value judgment in this category is futile. Teachers should examine their demands and expectations to determine whether they are being authoritarian and dictatorial. Teachers, in general, do not request unreasonable non-negotiable behaviors. They usually just want the students to do their work without disrupting the educational process of any other student and to accomplish this goal within a safe, caring environment. Most educators reasonably expect students to: (1) Do their schoolwork; (2) Not talk when the teacher is giving instructions; (3) Not disrupt other students; and (4) Not fight, hit, or torment other students.

Teachers have relatively few behaviors that they consider non-negotiable. Even within this area, students usually have a range of acceptable alternatives from which to choose. Moreover, teachers usually are willing to let students make the decisions when they demonstrate that they are capable of making good decisions. So don't be afraid to set some limits and to give clear directions to ensure that they are adhered to.

The following example illustrates a non-negotiable, "must" behavior. A kindergarten student has somehow escaped the confines of the fenced play-area and is standing in the middle of the busy street which is right off the school grounds. The teacher sees him and knows immediately that she must do something because she sees a car approaching the child at nearly 50 mph. Would she use any of the following communication patterns?

"How many times do I have to tell you to get out of the street?"

"If you don't come out of the street, you'll get run over."

"You are a bad boy for going into the street."

"If you keep up this type of behavior, you'll get hit just like your friend."

"I'll give you a sucker if you get out of the street."

"I want you to try to get out of the street."

"You know you make me very angry when you keep doing this."

"You should know better."

"Don't you ever let me catch you out in the street again."

"Think twice before you do something stupid like this again."

Would the teacher use ANY of these communication patterns in this situation? The answer is emphatically "NO!" She would, without a doubt, act immediately to take the child out of the street. She would tell him, "Don't you ever, and I mean EVER, go into that street again!" She would also do whatever was necessary to ensure that the child would not go into the street again.

If the child were to go into the street again the next day, would she say, "Oh, well, he's made his bed; he'll have to lie in it." or "I told him that would happen to him, and he should know better. Let him pay the consequences."? No, she wouldn't. In this life-or-death situation she would take whatever action was necessary to convince the child that he has no choice in the matter. She cares about him and loves him so much that she will not allow him to be unsuccessful, and she is willing to go to any extreme until he gets the message.

Furthermore, let's say for the sake of argument that this child talks back to the teacher, as though he were a teenager, with comments like: "Get off my back." "Your value system is archaic." "I *like* playing in the middle of the street." "You can't control my life." "All the other kids get to do it, and *their* parents don't care." "You're driving me crazy, ruining my personality, taking away all the fun in my life, and I'm going to run away."

If you were the teacher, what would you do? You would probably say, in effect, "That is not the point. The only thing that we are talking about is getting out of the street right now and staying out of the street." At times like this, adults do not worry about whether or not they are ruining the child's personality. They realize that if they don't take action and get the child out of the street, the child will be dead and they will not have to worry about his personality development.

Compare the actions and communication patterns in this life-and-death kindergarten example with what typically happens when a sixteen-year-old is flunking out of school, ditching, and starting to get into drugs. Teachers and parents don't always see this type of behavior as life-threatening and crucial. They don't see themselves as having the right to make the student go to school, pass his classes, and get off the drugs; and they use many of the indirect communication forms that they would never have thought of using in the previous example with the kindergartener in the street. They do not take an active and assertive stance to ensure the student's success, and they are much more susceptible to the student's manipulations.

To deal with this type of problem, it is important that both teachers and parents determine their priorities and clarify their own values so that they can communicate clearly to the student what is expected.

A teacher sought counseling after she came home early one day and caught her nine-year-old daughter smoking marijuana. She wanted professional advice about what she should do. When asked if her daughter's smoking marijuana was a problem to her, and whether or not she wanted her daughter to stop doing it, she said, "Well, I'm not real sure. I don't want my daughter sneaking around and doing it behind my back. Besides, I've been doing some reading on the subject, and I'm not sure if smoking marijuana isn't better than smoking cigarettes."

The counselor said, "Then your daughter's smoking marijuana is no problem to you, and your daughter will probably continue to smoke it."

She was somewhat taken aback, and asked what was meant. She was told that until she clearly decided that marijuana-smoking was a problem, her indecisiveness was a clear message to her daughter that it was okay to continue smoking marijuana. Once she clarified her own thinking and position on the subject—either seeing the smoking as a problem or not—then she could take appropriate action.

Any decision about what to do will be governed by this tautology: There is no problem until there is a problem. If parents or teachers are not willing to clarify their own values, positions, beliefs, and non-negotiable "must" behaviors, then—by omission—they are clearly communicating to the student that there is no problem. The adult must resolve the ambiguity in her own mind before she can proceed.

When teachers and parents are not successful at getting their students to do what they want them to do, it is because they have been using vague, indirect communication styles that reflect their underlying belief in the students' or their own incapabilities. By using direct, clear, effective communication patterns coupled with a belief that both the adults and the students are capable of doing what is required, teachers and parents will be better able to stop students from behaving inappropriately.

When teachers communicate their belief that the student is capable and clearly tell the student what is expected of him, they will resolve the majority of classroom discipline problems. Although there are no quantitative measures to substantiate this contention, it appears that these two simple intervention strategies alone can clear up 90-95% of the common discipline problems in schools. In the other 5-10% of the problems, simply believing that the student is capable and giving directions clearly and specifically will not stop inappropriate behavior. With this small percentage of problems, the teacher needs effective back-up strategies to convince the student that he must do what he is directed to do and that there is no way out. The next chapter discusses back-up strategies and interventions that can be utilized within the school environment.

# Chapter V:  Classroom Back-up Techniques

Once clear communication patterns have been established, it is important that teachers effectively back up their demands. In most cases a clear and specific demand will be effective. In some cases, however, a clear message does not work; in those cases the teacher must look for one of two possibilities. Either a strong, habitual belief-system on her part or on the student's part is at work, or an ineffective back-up technique is in use.

In the first case it is extremely important that the teacher see the student as capable and that any excuses or inappropriate belief-systems are eroded. If she sees the student as being capable, but the student has internalized the belief that he is incapable, then family counseling may be required to help both the student and the parents to discard their inappropriate beliefs. [This particular situation is dealt with in greater detail in the book *How to Deal with Difficult Discipline Problems: A Family-Systems Approach.*]

In the second case the teacher must develop effective back-up techniques to convey that she means what she says. The student must know that the inappropriate behavior will be stopped. Some students—especially students who have been out of control—will test the limits, even when given a clear message. Even though the teacher changes her own belief and sees the student as being capable of self-control, the student may not be convinced. The teacher must guarantee that the student does what is wanted by backing up her directives in a non-hostile, non-punishing way.

Back-up techniques are limited only by imagination and the specific situation. The teacher can begin to develop an effective back-up technique by asking herself these questions:

(1) What is the real problem to be solved? What is the goal? What behavior must the student do in order to be successful? (Stop stealing—or tell the truth about stealing? Do classwork—or go to detention?)

(2) How can I convey to the student that he must do the goal behavior? That I care about him and will not hurt him, belittle him, or punish him? That

I expect him to be successful? How can I convey to him that since I believe he is capable, I will not allow him to be anything less than successful?

To illustrate the structural principles of a good back-up technique, let us consider the following non-school-related example of a parental back-up technique. A sixteen-year-old girl tested the limits by staying out past her midnight curfew. Her father met her at the door and said, "I love you very much, and when I say, 'Be in the house by 12:00,' that is exactly what I mean. From now on, be in the house at 12:00, period. No excuses." Then he turned around and went to bed without further discussion, restriction, or punishment.

The next week the daughter was given permission to go out. When her date picked her up, the father followed them out to the car and got into the back seat. The daughter and her date looked at him in shock and asked what was going on.

The father said, "No problem. You weren't home by 12:00 last week, so this week I'll go along with you and see that you are home on time." He went with them. They were home by 12:00.

The next week the daughter wanted to go out again. The father said, "Fine. Do you wish to go on your own and be in the house by 12:00, or would you like me to come along to make sure that you are in by 12:00?" (The father gave the daughter a choice, but either option achieved the goal behavior. He did not give her a choice of being on time or being on restriction.) The daughter wanted to go out on her own and agreed to be in the house by 12:00.

The father said, "Fine. I love you and I trust you. See you at 12:00." She got the message that he meant what he said. He stuck with the goal, and he did not restrict nor punish her; he just made sure that she did the goal behavior.

In a school-related situation, a student was not going to Physical Education class or taking a shower. After determining the fact that it was important from both the school's and the family's perspectives that the student do both of these tasks, a back-up technique was devised. A teacher on his conference period, the custodian, the counselor, the school psychologist, and/or the vice-principal would meet the student at the end of the class period just before P.E. and escort him to P.E. At the end of the P.E. period, the P.E. teacher and any one of the previously mentioned school personnel would escort the student to the shower and say, "Would you like to take a shower on your own, or would you like us to help you to take a shower? Which would you like us to do?" The student chose to take a shower on his own. After two or three escorts to P.E., he decided that he could do the task on his own, and he never missed another P.E. class.

It is important to note that in a very small percentage of cases even carefully planned back-up techniques will be ineffective. In those cases either the student has not gotten the message that the teacher is serious and she must continue her efforts, or the parents are telling the student, either directly or indirectly, to continue the inappropriate behavior in school. In the latter case, since parents have more influence over a student than educators do, he will respond to the message of the parents.

For example, most school personnel have dealt with the problem of student fights. Sometimes the parents' message to the student is, "Don't ever start a fight, but defend yourself if anyone pushes you around. Stand up for yourself, and be a man." If the school's interventions are at variance with the parents' value system, the chances of stopping the behavior are greatly reduced. Therefore, teachers must work with and involve the parents of these students as soon as possible. (Three different levels of parental involvement to help resolve school-related discipline problems are discussed later in this chapter.)

Teachers must plan ahead for discipline problems as diligently as they plan their course material. Structured procedures to develop individual lesson-plans for specific students who act inappropriately and are hard to handle should be planned and implemented. A teacher who is prepared with appropriate intervention strategies will not make impractical or unrealistic statements in the heat of the moment (*e.g.,* "If you do that again, I'll kill you."), and they will have better, more systematic, and more effective back-up techniques.

In fact, educators must not only devise more systematic and well-thought-out plans for individual students, but they also must devise better school-wide discipline strategies.

Each teacher on campus should know what to do if a student acts inappropriately on the bus, on the playground, at lunch, or in the classroom. All faculty members should be prepared to take relatively similar action. Each teacher should have a general school-wide discipline plan, and know what to do if the student doesn't respond to initial interventions. The principal and the district administration need to back up teachers and make clear the mission of the school, what behavior is unacceptable on the student's part, and what action is expected from the teachers when students act inappropriately. Adequate preparation, clear delineation of roles and of expectations, and administrative support provide the foundation of staff morale. Unless teachers, the principal, and district administrators have united and well-planned discipline strategies, the educational institution is ill-equipped to deal with school-related discipline problems.

The staff must have policies, procedures, and behavioral rules which they will all support 100% of the time. Pre-planned back-up strategies to use in typical behavior problems will enable teachers to deal quickly and confidently with these problems.

As a staff, write down four or five non-negotiable school-wide rules that every student must follow and that every staff member must back up 100% of the time. Ask, "What district-level policies and procedures are necessary to back up these rules? What policies and/or procedures might need to be changed to make sure that these rules are being followed?" Devise back-up plans and strategies for your particular site so that everyone knows what to do in specific situations.

How would you respond if a consultant came to your campus and asked: "If a student did Behavior X, what would you do?" "Would you know what to do?" "Would the rest of the staff do something similar?" "Would your principal and your superintendent back you up?" "If the technique which you used did not work, what would you do next?" "If there were legal problems or issues involved, do you know what you can and cannot do?" "Again, would you be supported?"

If you don't know the answers to these and similar questions, it is time to develop a school-wide discipline and intervention plan as well as individual lesson-plans for specific students who are acting up in the classroom.

## Strategies and Interventions
## to Stop Inappropriate Classroom Behavior

### I. *State the Rules*

One of the first steps in setting up good classroom management is to state clearly the goals and the rules for the classroom. Classroom rules must be stated in very specific behavioral terms. The teacher should limit these rules to five or six top priorities that are absolutely necessary, that are non-negotiable, and which she is willing to back up every single time. She should operationally define her terms and keep them as behaviorally specific as possible. Instead of, "Pay attention and listen when I am giving instructions," she should say something like, "When I am giving instructions, stop everything that you are doing, look at me, and do absolutely no talking."

Once the rules are posted, the teacher will review them with the class so that everyone knows exactly what is expected. Many teachers send the rules home and require that the parents acknowledge that they have read them. The teacher should also include a paragraph stating that the parents agree with the rules, support the rules, and are willing to talk them over with the student, and are actively willing to help the teacher to ensure their child's compliance with the rules. A place for parents to provide telephone numbers at which they can be reached in order to help stop any problem immediately would reinforce the concept of co-operation.

Teachers generally require that the student does the assigned work, refrains from disrupting the educational process for other students, and does not physically or verbally harm himself or others. If the parents are not willing to support such reasonable rules, the teacher can probably anticipate problems in enforcing the rules with that particular student. In such cases, it is important that the counselor, school psychologist, or principal begin working with the parents immediately to help resolve any differences that exist between classroom rules and the family's value system before the school year starts.

## II. *Back Up the Rules*

After she has explained the rules to the students and the parents have signed a statement that they support her rules, the teacher must take certain steps to make sure that students behave appropriately in her classroom:

*Step 1. Say it clearly, and personalize it.* When giving individual directions to students, the teacher must state exactly what she wants them to do in specific, concrete terms. Instead of saying, "Okay, all you guys in the back of the classroom sit down," she must say, "John, Jim, Sue, and Tom, sit in your seats right now." Use of names personalizes the directives. Saying "right now" indicates when they are to act.

If the student sits in his seat but is either right back out of it again or he sits in it but does little work or acts inappropriately, she must amplify her directions. She might have to say, "Sit in your seat now, and stay there until I tell you to get out of it," or "Sit in your seat now, and while you are there keep your hands to yourself, keep your mouth shut, and do these ten problems neatly and correctly in the next fifteen minutes."

*Step 2. Close distance, and use non-verbal communications effectively.* If the students do not do what is requested of them, the teacher must walk over (close physical distance), confront the student who has the most influence (if she can control him, the rest of the students will follow), look him straight in the eye, and say, "John, sit in your seat right now." (Closing distance, calling the student by name, and making eye-contact when giving directions all intensify the power of the clear message.)

Some teachers say, "I don't want to have to go to the student. I'd be running around all over the place putting out fires. Besides, I have four or five kids who are always acting up. What then?" The point is that if the teacher takes the extra time early in the semester to get the class under control, she won't have to deal with the problem for the rest of the year. When she takes an active, firm stance to stop the "ring-leader" and she gets him under control, then she will have taken a big first step in controlling the rest of the classroom. The rest of the students will be saying to themselves, "If she means what she says and got him (our leader) under control, you know she will mean it with me." After she has established that she means what she says, then she probably will not have to close distance again to get the student to do what she wants.

When she closes distance and gives a clear verbal message to the student, she may also need to pay attention to other non-verbal signals. For example, she may need to control her tone of voice, her body posture, her facial expressions, and her gestures.

However, as the teacher closes distance and gives a clear message, the student may try to manipulate her. The student may protest that she always picks on him, that she doesn't like him, or that she's unfair. He might pout, argue, cry, ask "Why me?", or question her authority. These manipulations have nothing to do with the target behavior (*e.g.,* sitting in his seat right now). The teacher must refuse to discuss any side issues and insist that he sit in his seat immediately.

*Step 3. Stick to the main issue.* The teacher must use the "broken record" technique: she acts as if she were stuck in a groove and repeats her demand ("Sit in your seat now.") over and over again. She might say, "I know that is the way you feel (acknowledging and respecting the student's feelings), but that is not the *point.* Sit in your seat right now." If the student does not go to his seat after she has said this and intensified the message two or three times, then she must go to Step 4. If this is a student who has a long history of difficulty and many other interventions have already been tried, say it once and then go to Step 4 immediately.

*Step 4. The student needs your help.* The teacher takes the student by the elbow and physically escorts him to his seat and places him in his seat. A less direct method would be to give the student a choice in the matter by saying something like, "You may choose to go to your seat right now on your own and get to work, or you may choose to have me help you go to your seat and get to work. Which would you prefer?" She gives the student a choice but not a way out. If he gives you the teacher any trouble or talks back, this is a clear message to you that he needs your help to put him in his seat.

If the student says, "You touch me, and I'll sue you", or if the teacher is physically afraid of him and doesn't think that she could make him sit in his seat, she has three options:

(a) If she anticipates such a problem, she can ask other teachers or the principal to stand outside the door. (Please see pre-planned individual student discipline plan: Worksheet I, on page 92.) If the student refuses to follow a clear directive, the other adults enter and help the student to sit in his seat and get to work. If the student resists this effort, the teacher or the principal can remove the student from the room until the classroom teacher can set up a teacher/parent structured conference (Level One of parental involvement, which will be discussed later in this chapter).

A school can develop teams of school personnel (lunch aides, classroom aides, custodians, teachers on planning periods, vice-principals, and others.) who would be on call during certain pre-designated periods of the day. Any time that a teacher needed help and had not worked out a pre-planned intervention, she could use a pre-arranged signal (*e.g.,* a telephone call to the office) to summon the team to her room to remove the student until she could call the parents to resolve the problem.

(b) If the student refuses to sit in his seat and there is no pre-planned back-up support from other teachers or the principal, the teacher should turn on a tape-recorder, which she has ready to go, and say, "I'm turning on this tape-recorder, John, so that when we have our parent conference your parents will know exactly what I said and did and exactly what you said and did. I care about you, and I want you to get a good education. Now sit down in your seat and get to work right now. (If no response:) Here; let me take you by the arm and escort you to your seat." Once he is in his seat, say, "I'm leaving this tape-recorder on, by your desk, so that when your parents come in they will also know what went on while you were working. Do these ten problems neatly and correctly in the next fifteen minutes. Raise your hand if you finish before that time. Absolutely no talking. Start right now." If the student refuses during this procedure, the teacher must escort him to the principal's office until she has time to call the parents and set up a conference. If she can't leave her class and she can't get anyone to cover her class or come to her room to pick up the student, then she can take her whole class on a creative field-trip to the principal's office. ("Forty of you will go to the office; thirty-nine will return.") She must do whatever it takes to convince the student that she means what she says, that there is no way out, and that she will not allow him to mess up in her classroom.

(c) If the teacher thinks that the parents might sue, she should call and talk to them before she initiates her intervention plan. She should tell the parents that she doesn't believe in hurting or punishing students, but, because she cares about their child, she expects him to do his work and to be successful in her class. She would like their permission to take him by the arm and place him in his seat the next time he does not sit down when she asks him to do so. If they give their permission, then she should have them tell the student so that he knows that she and the parents are working together. (A note of caution: Check with your school district. Some districts need to have the parents give permission in writing.) On the other hand, if they say that they will sue, she should reaffirm to the parents that she cares about their youngster and that she wants him to get the best possible education. In her class, however, students must do their work and behave properly. Since their child will not follow directions and she doesn't have parental permission to make him sit in his seat and get to work, then they need to come to school and make him do his work. If they come to school and they make him behave, there is no problem. If they come to school and they can't get the student to behave, then there is a problem and the family should be referred to the school counselor or school psychologist for a family counseling session. If the parents refuse to come to

## WORKSHEET I.: INDIVIDUAL DISCIPLINE LESSON-PLAN

Student's Name_____ _____Telephone Number_____

Review of previous records for pertinent information:

Description of inappropriate behavior (in specific behavioral terms):

First intervention strategy:

Anticipated student response to intervention:

Second intervention strategy:

Anticipated student response to intervention:

Third intervention strategy:

Anticipated student response to intervention:

Fourth intervention strategy:

Anticipated student response to intervention:

Fifth intervention strategy:

Anticipated student response to intervention:

Other teachers' or principal's suggestions for interventions (Team approach—get some ideas from other professionals.):

Worksheet I  cont.

Development of back-up support:

General plan:  (If initial interventions do not work, what do you need to do in order to back them up to make the student be successful? Whom do you need to help you? Develop a plan with them and get their okay for support.)

_____ OK from principal

_____ OK from other teachers

_____ OK from counselor

_____ OK from parents

_____ OK from other school personnel (librarian, bus driver, custodian, lunch aides, etc.)

Further action needed:

_____ Referral to counselor

_____ Referral to principal

_____ Parent conference

Resolution of problem:

school and support the teacher, then, again, they should be referred to either the counselor or the school psychologist for a family counseling session (Level Two of parental involvement, which will be discussed later in this chapter), or they should be referred to the principal for a parent/school conference (Level Three of parental involvement, which will also be discussed later in this chapter).

Don't fly by the seat of your pants; have everything planned out. If necessary, have everything written out on an individual lesson-plan on which you anticipate the student's behavior and prepare for it. (Worksheet I has an outline of an "Individual Discipline Lesson-plan".)

If a teacher has an on-going discipline problem with a particular student, she should take some time and plan out a systematic intervention strategy before the next battle begins. To help plan she might talk the problem over with other teachers and brainstorm for possible intervention and back-up techniques that focus on the real problem. She should anticipate the student's possible reactions to various interventions and then plan contingent interventions and back-ups for each of those responses. She should also ask the principal for suggestions, as well as find out what support she can count on from him in implementing the total program. She needs to establish clear limits: at a certain point she must draw the line and do nothing more without getting the parents involved.

The types of intervention and back-up options in the school setting depend upon the creativity of the teacher and the staff and upon the teacher's personal limits of time and energy.

One teacher told a junior-high student to go to math class. The student refused. The teacher said, "You have no choice, so go to class now."

The student said, "NO!" and tried to run away.

The teacher went after him and caught him. (Many teachers would not do this, but it is a clear message to the student that he will not run away.) The student said that he wouldn't go to class, broke loose, ran into the teachers' lounge, and wrapped himself around a chair so that the teacher couldn't take him. The teacher repeated the directive and gave the student a choice: He could go to class on his own, or the teacher would take him to class. The student, yelling out his indignation, refused (a clear message to the teacher that the student needed help). The teacher then picked up the student and the chair and started to walk to math class with them. As they started to get into the mainstream of other students going to class, the student said, "Put me down; I'll go to class." The teacher put him down and escorted him to math class. The student went to math class the rest of the semester and passed the course. He got the message.

Some teachers would not be willing to go this far, and no one suggests that they should. Depending on their temperment, time, and energy, some teachers willingly try four, five, or six intervention back-up options before they involve the parents. Others are willing to go only as far as one or two options. The number of options attempted doesn't matter. What matters is (1) that teachers have planned their interventions and know the limit to which they will go before involving the parents, and (2) that they use back-up techniques which emphasize that there is no way out of doing the goal behavior and which convince the student that he must do the goal behavior. (Other examples of teacher back-up techniques will be given in Chapter VI.)

Some teachers say, "What happens if the student is bigger than I am, or if he has a violent temper or a weapon?" Teachers should not do anything unplanned or anything that will get them hurt. If a student has a weapon, the teacher must get help. The following story illustrates an effective approach. A petite teacher in an inner-city school was frightened (and reasonably so) by a big hostile male student who had been kept back a few times. Although she was clear and assertive, she was afraid that she could not physically back up her demands if it came to that. She decided to implement her new program of getting her students back under control with the pre-planned assistance of the principal and another male teacher outside her door. The next day when she clearly stated what behavior she expected, the student challenged her. When he did, the principal and the other male teacher walked into the room and took the student out of her class, clearly indicating to the other students—as well as to the boy himself—that this type of behavior would no longer be tolerated. They called the boy's parents and set up a conference.

A teacher should never put her safety in jeopardy. She should plan ahead—but, again, she should clearly state her expectations and convince her students that she means what she says and that she will do whatever it takes to make sure that they act appropriately.

When teacher back-up techniques are not working (whether it is after the first intervention or the tenth one) and the teacher has reached her personal limit, the next step is to bring in the parents for a structured teacher/parent conference (Level One of parental involvement). At this conference the teacher asks the parents to help solve the problem.


III. *Structured Parent Conference*

All teachers should operate under the assumption that the parents care and want to help solve the problem. Maintaining a positive attitude, the teacher sees herself and the parents working together as a team. At this conference, teacher, parents, and *student* meet for a short, highly structured meeting. The student must be present at the conference so that he can hear that his teacher and his parents are working as a team. This meeting very often does not last more than five to ten minutes. Again, everything must be planned out ahead

WORKSHEET II: STRUCTURED PARENT/TEACHER/STUDENT
CONFERENCE


Student's Name _____

Date and Time of Incident _____


1. STUDENT'S STRENGTHS AND SUCCESSES: Give a brief general progress-report on the student and relate some positive aspects of the student's school performance.




2. PROBLEM AREA: Description of the student's inappropriate behavior. What was actually said and done?—(the what, when, and where.) Use specific, concrete, behavioral terms. (Out of seat, hitting others—rather than poor attitude, hyperactive, immature, etc.).




3. ATTEMPTS TO RESOLVE THE SITUATION: Describe what you did in response to the student's inappropriate behavior. Be as accurate as possible and describe exactly what you said and did to stop the inappropriate behavior. Also, describe how the student responded to you.




4. INTENDED GOAL: What you want to accomplish with the parents.




Examples of intended goals:
    A. "Parents have more power than teachers in getting children to do what they want them to do when they clearly state their demands.
    "I know that you care about _____ and, therefore, want him to succeed. Are you willing to make a demand to him that he:
_____?"

Worksheet II cont.

B. "I have told _____ not to _____
_____ . Parents have more power to stop
behaviors than teachers have. Would you be willing to demand that _____
stop _____ ? Would you be willing to tell him that now?"

C. Write out your own request for the parents.

## 5. SUMMARY OF PARENTAL RESPONSE TO REQUEST:

Checklist:

A. _____ Parents were very supportive and gave clear demand messages to stop the inappropriate behavior.

B. _____ Parents were supportive but gave vague, unclear messages. When this fact was pointed out to them, they made clear demands.

C. _____ Parents were not willing to support the school intervention.

D. Comments:

## 6. PLANNED INTERVENTION:

A. _____ Parents are willing to tell student over the phone to stop the inappropriate behavior. Phone numbers where the parents can be reached: Home: _____ Work: _____ .

B. _____ Parents are also willing to come to school to demand that the student behave and will stay to back up their demand if needed.

C. _____ Conflict between the school and the parents. Referral to the school counselor or school psychologist for family counseling session.

D. _____ Conflict between the school and the parents. Referral to the principal for school/parent conference.

of time. The teacher should write down exactly what the student did and what she did in response to that behavior. (See Worksheet II: Structured Parent/Teacher/Student Conference.) She should also write down what she expects from the parents. When talking to the parents, she must communicate in very concrete behavioral terms ("He got out of his seat and hit John. When I told him to sit in his seat, stay there, and never hit anyone again in this classroom, he told me. . . ."—instead of "He is rebellious and has a poor attitude.").

Here are some general guidelines to follow when contacting the parents to set up this conference:

(1) The teacher should speak positively and clearly. She should stress that she knows that the parents are equally concerned and will want to work with her in resolving the problem.

(2) She should focus on the main reasons for the call. If necessary, she can use the "broken record" technique with the parents when requesting exactly what she wants from them (attending the conference) and being specific about the need to resolve the problem behavior (out of seat, hitting others, etc.). She should not allow the parents to sidetrack her to other issues, such as her teaching ability.

(3) She should have at least three alternate times and dates available when she would be willing to meet with the parents. In general, it is better to meet with the parents at school. Parents can take time off from work to go to the doctor because it is important; they can take time off from work to see their child's teacher because *it is important.* The teacher should stress the importance of meeting as quickly as possible in order to resolve the problem now, so that their child can get back on the track to being successful at school. At this point, she will give the parents a choice of two of the available times when she can meet with them. In a positive, matter-of-fact way she should promote one of these two times. She can keep the third appointment-time open as a last option.

(4) The teacher should not become hostile, critical, or defensive. Even if they challenge her or tell her that she is not a good teacher or even worse, she must try to stay positive. The teacher must stay calm and refocus the parents' concerns about her ability onto the goal behavior (meeting with the parents and solving the student's inappropriate behavior). If need be, because the parents keep challenging you on a personal level, use the "broken record" technique, indicating to the parents that you understand that that is the way they feel, but the issue at hand, right now, is the need to solve the student's behavioral problem, so when can we meet to solve this problem? Immediately give them a choice of the two meeting times available.

(5) The teacher should neither apologize for bothering them nor minimize the problem (NOT: "I probably shouldn't have called you about this, but we

## WORKSHEET III: PARENTS TELEPHONE CONFERENCE

How to contact parents for a conference:

Speak positively and clearly, stressing the fact that you know that *the parents are equally concerned and will want to work with you in resolving the problem with their child.*

Stay on track (broken record), requesting exactly what you want from them (attending the conference) and being specific about the problem behavior (out of seat, hitting others, etc.).

Have at least three times and dates ready so that you know when you can meet with them.

Don't get defensive, be hostile, or blame the parent.

Don't apologize for bothering them, and don't minimize the problem (NOT: "I probably shouldn't have called you about this, but we are having a minor difficulty with Jane. . . .").

Don't minimize the consequences of the student's behavior. (Instead of "I don't know what is going to happen if she continues to show up late to class and does not do her work," say, "Jane will fail my course unless she does her work and is on time to my class.")

Don't allow the parents to convince you to meet separately (without the child's presence), or you will defeat your purposes.

List the following before calling the parents:

1. The inappropriate behavior of the student: (What he/she did—in behavioral terms.)


2. What you did and said:


3. What you want from the parents (to attend a conference to solve the problem):


4. Times and dates when you can meet with the family:

   (a)

   (b)

   (c)

are having a minor problem with Jane. . . ."). She must tell the parents that this is an important issue, and that she is glad to have the opportunity to work with the parents to solve this problem before it gets out of hand and interferes seriously with the student's chances of becoming successful.

(6) Neither should she minimize the consequences of the student's behavior. Instead of saying, "I don't know what's going to happen if she continues to show up late for class and does not do her work," the teacher should say something like, "Jane will fail my course unless she gets to class on time and does her work. I know that you care about your daughter and want her to be successful in school. Would you prefer that we meet to solve this problem on Tuesday at 7:30 before school or on Wednesday at 3:30 when school gets out?"

(7) To have a successful conference, the teacher cannot allow the parents to exclude (or excuse) the student from attending it. (Worksheet III is a summary of guidelines to use when contacting parents and an outline to use in preparing for the telephone conference.)

If, when you call the parents, they are initially reluctant to come to the conference, remember to stay positive, and use your broken-record technique to get them to come to the conference. If they say that they can't come because they work, indicate that you know it is difficult but that the problem is very important. Further state that you know that if all of you work together as a team, there is a good chance that the problem can be solved quickly and then the parents won't have to be bothered at work again. Then say, "When can we meet, Tuesday at 7:30 a.m., or Wednesday at 3:30 p.m.?" If they say that they will lose their job, indicate your willingness to call or write to their employer to make sure that he knows how important it is, and that if you all work together the problem can be resolved quickly. Repeat your question, "So when can we meet, Tuesday at 7:30 a.m., or Wednesday at 3:30 p.m.?"

If they challenge you and say, "I don't have any problems with my child at home. I can't see why you can't control him in school. That's what you are paid for," don't get defensive. Turn this statement into the positive and to your advantage by saying, "That's really great that you are such a successful parent and that you have no problems with him at home. I'm sure that if we meet, you can show me how you have successfully gotten him to do what you want, and we can solve this problem here at school so that he can be back on track to being successful. When can we meet, Tuesday at 7:30 a.m., or Wednesday at 3:30 p.m.?" Again, do whatever it takes, but get the parents in to see you. When the parents agree to a conference, you are ready to go to the structured conference. (In Worksheet IV, on page 102, there are examples of typical situations that might arise when you call the parents for a structured parent/teacher/student conference. Plan ahead and work out what your responses will be.)

Usually, teachers ask, "What happens when the parents say that they will come to the conference and then never show up—what then?" Generally, this happens with a rather small percentage of parents. However, if they do not show up, the teacher must give them the benefit of the doubt the first time and try to reschedule immediately. At this time, the teacher must insist that a meeting be scheduled within 24 hours. If the parents refuse or do not show up for the second scheduled meeting, the student should be suspended to parental supervision until the teacher can meet with them to solve the problem. This suspension is designed to pressure the parents into attending a meeting, not to cure the student's inappropriate behavior. If the parents have no phone, the teacher or some other designated school personnel must either make a home visit or send a registered letter to get the parents to come to the meeting. She must do whatever is necessary to increase the student's chances of being successful.

When the teacher meets with the parents, she should have everything planned, written out (at least in outline form) and ready to go (See Worksheet II, on page 96.) Her preparation may even include her tape-recording of what actually was said and done in the classroom. The teacher should start the conference with a general progress-report and stress some positive aspects of the student. After this very brief introduction, she should get right to the business at hand and go through the four-step structured parent/teacher/student conference.

*Step 1. State the problem in behavioral terms.* "I have been having difficulty in getting John to stop using profanity in school. This is what he said. . . . This is what I said and did about it. . . ."

The teacher must say exactly what the student did and said. Parents need to know, so that they can take appropriate action to correct the problem—if it is a problem to them.

*Step 2. Solicit parental support.* Never tell parents what inappropriate behavior the student did (Step 1) and then turn the meeting over to them for a response. This is like saying, "Well, what are you going to do about this terrible kid? Please give me some ideas and suggestions right now." This puts the parents on the spot and usually makes them somewhat defensive. Instead of putting them on the spot, take the active role in the meeting and let the parents know what actions you would like them to take to help to correct the problem. Tell them what you want and see if they will do it. The important part of this process is telling the parents exactly what you need and want from them, and then *asking* the parents if they are *willing* to take an active stance to stop the behavior. Never tell or demand that they do what you've asked. Always phrase your request so you are asking them if they are *willing* to help. Examples of this are as follows:

## WORKSHEET IV: ROLE-PLAY SITUATIONS—
## CALLING THE PARENTS FOR A PARENT/TEACHER CONFERENCE

*Remember: Stay with the goal; use the broken-record technique; do not get defensive; and work together as a team.*

SITUATION #1:  You call the mother at work and ask to have a conference. She says that she can't meet with you because she has to work. What do you say to her?

   *Response:*

SITUATION #2:  You call home and ask the parents to come to school for a conference. The father tells you that they have no problem with their child at home. "Why can't you handle him at school? Isn't that what we pay you for?" What is your response?

   *Response:*

SITUATION #3:  You call home for a conference. The parent says, "Just leave it to me. I will take care of the problem and punish him." What do you say?

   *Response:*

SITUATION #4: You call home for a conference. The parent says, "We spank him at home, and that works. Why don't you just spank him at school?" They give their permission. What do you say?

*Response:*

SITUATION #5: Either one of the following happens: (1) No one ever answers the phone when you call,or (2) You find out that there is no phone in the home. What do you do?

*Response:*

SITUATION #6: You set up a parent conference—and the parents don't show up. What do you do?

*Response:*

SITUATION #7: Along with your staff, identify two or three typical situations involving parents in your area. As a group, do some brainstorming and decide what you might say and do for each situation.

*Response:*

"Parents have more power in getting students to do what they want when they clearly state their demands. I know that you care about John and, therefore, want him to succeed. Are you willing to demand that the profanity stop?" or "I have told John not to cuss in class ever again. He continues to cuss. Parents have more power to stop behaviors than teachers do. Would you be willing to demand that John never cuss in my class again? Would you tell him that now?"

*Step 3. Have parents make the demand during the conference.* If the parents are willing to support you, have them give a clear demand right there in the session so that the student knows you are working together as a team. The teacher monitors the parent's demand to make sure that it is not phrased as a punishment-contract, or as a threat. If the parent threatens, the teacher must point out that he or she is giving a choice and that she would prefer a clear demand to stop the behavior. For example, if the father says, "John, you know how upset this makes your mother and me. If you don't stop this behavior, you'll be on restriction for a month." The teacher might say, "What I heard you say is that it is okay for him to cuss in my class as long as he is willing to be on restriction for a month. I would prefer a clear statement that he is never to cuss in my class again. Are you willing to tell him that? Would you please do it now?"

(Review Chapter II on Indirect Messages. A summary of indirect communication patterns is provided in Worksheet V, on page 105, so that you can quickly review them. Practice-exercises for responses to indirect messages given by parents during the structured parent/teacher/student conference are provided in Worksheet VI, on page 106, so that teachers can be prepared to respond to parental indirect messages.)

*Step 4. Refer the case to a school counselor or make a parental contract for support.*

(a) If the teacher meets with great resistance from the parents (*e.g.,* value conflicts or significant lack of parenting skills), she should refer the parents to the counselor or the school psychologist for a family counseling session (Level Two of parental involvement) to help resolve the problem.

(b) If the parents support the teacher and give a clear demand to the student to stop the inappropriate behavior, then the teacher should ask for telephone numbers at which she can reach them at any time. This is done so that in the unlikely event that this problem should ever occur again, the teacher can either take or send John to the office, where she or one of the office staff can call the parents and have the parents reinforce their demand to the student over the telephone to do what is requested by the teacher. The teacher then has the parents indicate that if this telephone procedure does not stop the inappropriate behavior, whether one of them would be willing to

## WORKSHEET V: REVIEW-LIST
## FOR INDIRECT COMMUNICATION PATTERNS

1. Ignore the behavior—hoping that it will go away.
2. Encourage the behavior—"Do that again. I dare you."
3. Honesty about symptom—"Just tell me the truth about it."
4. Concern about symptom—"Aren't you even sorry you did it?"
5. Facing the problem—"If you will just face up to the problem!"
6. Effort to change—"If you will just make an effort—try!"
7. Willingness to discuss reasons—"Tell me why you did it."
8. Thinking about behavior—"Just think before you act."
9. Willingness to learn and/or to accept help—"Learn from it." "You need to get motivated."
10. Don't get caught—"Just don't ever let me catch you doing that again."
11. Abstract, meaningless directions—"Use common sense." "Don't give the teacher too hard a time." "Grow up."
12. Statements of fact—"I see you didn't bring your papers and pencils to class again."
13. Classification systems—"You're a bad boy."
14. Questions—"How many times do I have to tell you?"
15. Predictions—"You'll flunk out of school."
16. If/Then Contracts and punishments—"If you do that one more time, I'll. . . ." (This statement tells the student that it is okay to misbehave if he is willing to pay the price.)
17. Wishes, wants, and shoulds—"I wish you wouldn't." "I want you to. . . ." "You should know better."
18. Reasoning, inspiring, explaining, long lectures—"You've heard this all before, but. . . ."
19. Non-verbal comments about behavior—

    (a) Incongruent positive non-verbals—smiling, affection, nodding head, and so forth.

    (b) Indirect messages—locks on doors, surveillance, unbreakable furniture, and so forth.

## WORKSHEET VI: RESPONSES FOR TEACHERS TO THE INDIRECT MESSAGES GIVEN BY PARENTS DURING THE STRUCTURED PARENT/TEACHER CONFERENCE

### PRACTICE WORKSHEET

Teachers need to be prepared to respond to parents' indirect messages during the structured parent/teacher conference. You should commit to memory the typical indirect communication patterns listed in Table V.

After the teacher has requested that the parents give clear, direct demand messages to the child during the conference, it is important to listen very intently to see if the parents actually give a clear message to stop the inappropriate behavior. When the parents give a typical non-demand message, the teacher needs to be empathic, respectful, and caring for the parents' position, but must also objectively and firmly indicate to the parents that they have not told the student to stop the inappropriate behavior. Rather, they have given a choice of whether or not to stop the behavior.

This exercise will give you some practice in developing responses to typical indirect parental demands.

Write a response to each of these parental statements that challenges the statement and requests the parents to give a clear demand to the student.

1. "Now, John, you know how angry and upset your mother and I get when you act this way. We've talked to you many times before about this. If you don't stop, you are going to be on restriction."

Teacher's response:

2. "I wish you would try to act like a human being just once in your life. You need to learn that you can't just do what you want to do. How long do your mother and I have to put up with this type of behavior?"

Teacher's response:

3. "Listen, Buster, you've got no TV, no phone, no friends, no car, and no dates—nothing—until you get your homework done and your grades up."

Teacher's response:

4. "You should know better than this. If you don't get a good education, you'll never get anywhere in this world. You know how important education is these days. You should be ashamed that you are not working up to your potential."

Teacher's response:

come to class to sit with John, tell him clearly and specifically to behave, and then make sure that he does his work and acts appropriately. (The teacher must do whatever it takes to convince John that he must behave; there is no way out.) If the parents confirm all these requests, thank them for their support and for working together with the school as a team to insure the best education possible for their son, and end the conference. Again, if the parents are not willing to support the school, a referral to the counselor or psychologist is made.

The following example illustrates how this structured parent/teacher/student conference strategy can intervene to stop further inappropriate behavior. A counselor was asked to take over a junior-high-school special-education class for a few minutes. One of the students in the class started arguing with another student. The counselor stepped between the students before the confrontation became physical (Intervention One), took a firm stance, and told them to sit down and get to work immediately (Intervention Two). One student refused and wanted to continue the confrontation with the other student. At this point, the belligerent student was physically placed in his seat (Intervention Three). He was told to open his book and get to work immediately (Intervention Four). With anger and defiance, the student said that he would not do it and that no one could make him do it (manipulations). Nose-to-nose with him (Intervention Five), the counselor told him to get to work immediately (Intervention Six). Again, he refused. The counselor took out the student's book, opened it to the proper page, placed a pencil in the student's hand (Intervention Seven), and told him, again, to work on his assignment, and to do it neatly and correctly (Intervention Eight).

The student looked at the counselor and said, "I'm not going to do it, and you are going to have to move my hand to write every answer if you think you are going to get me to do this." At this point, the counselor had reached his personal limit of teacher-oriented interventions with this student, and he told the teacher's aide to watch the class for a few minutes so that he could take the student to the office (Intervention Nine). When they reached the office, the counselor called the student's grandmother, based on an agreement reached during a previously held grandparent/counselor/student conference. (The parents had abandoned the boy.) The counselor told the grandmother exactly what the student and he had said and done up to that point. He asked her if she would be willing to tell her grandson, specifically and clearly, that he was to do what was requested of him (Intervention Ten). She said that she would be glad to do so. Whatever she said to the student over the phone worked because he immediately began to act more appropriately.

At the end of their conversation, the student handed the phone to the counselor and said, "Here; my grandmother would like to speak to you." The grandmother said that she was coming to school and would be there in half an hour to make sure that he acted appropriately for the rest of the day. The counselor thanked her for her support, and escorted the student back to class—where he sat down and began to work slowly and reluctantly. The grandmother came to class later, told the boy exactly what he was to do and how he was to behave, and stayed with him at school until he completed all of his work for that day, neatly and accurately. He got the message that the school would not put up with inappropriate behavior.

Under most situations, having the parents in class to stop inappropriate behavior is very effective. However, once in a while this technique does not work out well. In such cases, the problem is either (1) that the parents are not sure what is expected of them while they are in the classroom; (2) that they have belief-systems under which either they feel that they can't control the child or the child can't control himself; or (3) that (in very rare situations) they don't have good parenting skills.

In the first situation this problem can be resolved with a short in-service training session given to the parents before they go into the classroom on what they should say and do if their child acts up. This session will help to clarify the role of the parents in the classroom and what is expected from them. As a staff, or district, you can develop guidelines for parents and have them available for every parent who comes onto the campus. You could have in-service meetings to train and inform teachers and parents in how to use this approach—a technique which would also reduce the uncertainty. Another option to this solution is to develop a videotape presentation modeling and explaining the roles which the parents should take in the classroom.

In the other two previously mentioned situations in which the parents are ineffective in the classroom, they will have to be referred to the school psychologist or counselor to have them work with the parents to see if they can help to resolve the difficulties.

The variety of back-up techniques available within the school setting is limited only by the imagination of educators. It is important to remember, however, to focus on getting the students to do the goal behavior, not on punishing them. If the clear goal-directed demands don't work, and the teacher's non-punishing back-ups don't work, then she has to get the parents involved.

The first step in parental involvement is the short, structured parent/ teacher/student conference. This strategy of parental support as a back-up technique for the teacher usually works very well. However, as stated before, at times this method doesn't work—either because the parents believe that they are not in control of their child or because they do not wish to support the teacher. In either case, if the structured parent/teacher conference and/or the parent telephone call or classroom visit does not work, and if the school has a counselor or a school psychologist trained in this method, the teacher should refer the parents for a family counseling session (Level Two of parental involvement).

At this second stage of parental involvement, the counselor or school psychologist can clarify any of the parents' value conflicts with the school (*e.g.,* parents telling the child to fight); erode the inapppropriate beliefs about why the student is misbehaving; help to convince the parents that they are very successful and capable of changing the student's behavior if they wish to do so; and help to coach them in back-up strategies that will help the teacher and make the student successful in class. This family-counseling stage is crucial for the small percentage of students who resist all of the teacher's efforts. (These counseling interventions are beyond the scope of this book but are developed in *How to Deal with Difficult Discipline Problems: A Family Systems Approach.*)

By the end of the counseling session, the counselor should know whether or not the parents are going to support the teacher and the school in stopping the inappropriate behavior and whether they are willing to follow through with parental back-ups that will ensure school success. If the parents are not going to support the school, no matter what the reason, the counselor will be empathic and supportive, but will point out to the parents that their actions are a clear message to their child to continue to act inappropriately at school. By focusing on parental responsibility, this maneuver forces the parents to decide and to state whether they support the teacher or do not support her.

If the parents are in conflict with the school and are not willing to support the teacher, and if the counselor can't help them to resolve the problem, then the counselor should refer them to the principal, or to a district-level administrator, for the purpose of holding a school/parent conference (Level Three of parental involvement). This particular counselor-based referral to the school principal is different from a teacher-based referral to the principal. The teacher-based referrals are the more traditionally made referrals in which the intent of the meeting is to have the principal or vice-principal exert his/her power and influence to stop the individual student's inappropriate behavior. The counselor-based referral to the principal, made only after all other options have been tried, is, in a sense, the school's final effort to force the parents to make a stand. The proceedings should be fairly legalistic, formal, and tape-recorded. At this crucial juncture the school administrative personnel have to explore their philosophies, policies, and procedures to decide if they are going to tolerate the problem in the hope that by doing their best and trying the same things that they have been trying for years, that things will get better; or whether they will take a firm, assertive stance and give the parents three choices:

(1) The parents can work together with the school to give the student a clear demand message that he must behave and then back up their demands so

that he is successful. (Some parents of high-school students actually escort their children from class to class to stop truancy, fights, inappropriate classroom behavior, and so on.);

(2)  They can check the student out of the school and put him into a school where they allow that type of behavior. (Some parents move their children out of states which require their students to attend school until they are 18 and into one of the states which require attendance only until age 16.);

(3)  They can sign a document that states: (a) They take full responsibility for their child's inappropriate behavior. They will not help the teacher to stop the inappropriate behavior because they value that behavior and actively encourage the behavior; (b) They will take full responsibility for the student's academic, social, and emotional failure within the school; (c) They will be responsible for all legal and economic liabilities for their child's inappropriate behavior and his/her probable school failure; and (d) They realize that the school will not allow their child to disrupt the educational process of other students and that their child will be suspended to *parental supervision* at the first sign of any disruptive behavior.

Section 3(d) works especially well for parents who work and who say that they can't or won't help the teacher. The educational code (at least in the State of California) requires that suspension must be to parental supervision; therefore, if they don't supervise their children, the school district can if it wishes file suit against them and have them taken to court. To increase parental motivation, tell them that local authorities will make unscheduled visits to their home to ensure that the parents are at home supervising their child.

At this point, if the parents are still not willing to work with the school or with the teacher, whether or not they sign the document the administrators have enough information to take them to court if necessary. It is not likely to proceed this far; most parents will work with a teacher and/or school counselor or psychologist, especially if she can convince them that she is genuinely interested in their child's well-being and is willing to respect them and to work with them, as a team, in order to help resolve differences and the student's inappropriate behavior in school.

As a summary, Worksheet VII presents an outline of the ideas which have been presented in this chapter.

WORKSHEET VII: OUTLINE FOR CLASSROOM MANAGEMENT

## I. CLASSROOM STANDARDS SHEET

Rules of the classroom are clearly stated, and all students and their parents are required to sign the sheet. The sheet includes a provision whereby, if after repeated demands the teacher has been unable to get the desired behavior, the parent agrees to talk to the student on the phone or come to school to demand the appropriate behavior.

## II. DEALING WITH BEHAVIOR PROBLEMS

A. Decide on the specific behaviors of the student that are to be changed. Start with the most important behavior. As you are successful with one or two of the most important behaviors, the rest will follow.

1. Make the goal clear and specific (*e.g.,* continually out of his seat without permission *vs.* he has an attitude problem). Avoid vague terms such as depressed, moody, stubborn, contrary, willful.

2. Avoid conflicting goals such as trying, learning, wanting to, lying.

3. Break the goal into manageable units.

If the goal is to complete the math assignment, say, "Do these five problems first. Do them neatly and correctly and have them finished in the next five minutes. Raise your hand if you finish before then, and I will check them for you."

4. Monitor behavior to ensure the student's success. If the student is not successful, that is a clear message to you that he needs more structure, that the tasks need to be broken down more, and that his behavior has to be monitored more closely with appropriate back-up techniques in order to keep him on task.

B. Obstacles to clear demands:
   1. Am I sure that he/she is capable of this behavior?
   a. What possible "excuse" for him/her have I been entertaining?
   b. What beliefs of incapability have I been entertaining?

2. Am I sure that this is a reasonable and essential goal?

a. Is this a must, non-negotiable behavior that is necessary to: (1) the child's well-being, (2) other students' well-being, and (3) my well-being?

b. Am I willing to put in the time and the energy needed to follow through on reaching this goal? (*e.g.,* monitoring the student's behavior, calling the parents if repeated demands do not work, etc.)

3. Does this student manipulate me? How might I deal with this possibility? How will I avoid the trap of arguing? Develop an individual behavior lesson plan; develop back-ups and various alternatives; prepare and role play for any eventuality.

4. Do I have a weakness for a particular behavior because I engaged in it as a child?

C. Demonstrating to student a 100% commitment to changing the behavior:

1. Clear statement of rule (demands *vs.* threats, explanations, etc.): "Sit in your seat now, and stay there until the bell rings."

2. If behavior continues, demand can be reiterated (broken-record technique), or parent contact can be initiated with immediate phone call.

a. Parent can be contacted via parent-contact form sent to school counselor or vice-principal. Parent is asked to talk to student or come to school to make the demand that the student behave appropriately.

b. An alternative to immediate contact with the parent is a request for a parent/teacher/student conference.

(1) Conference steps:

(a) Mention a strong point of the student.

(b) Statement of behavior goal:

"I have been having difficulty in getting _____ to stop using profanity in school."

(c) Soliciting parental support to give a clear demand that the student stop the inappropriate behavior.

"Parents have more power in getting children to do what they want them to do when they clearly state their demands. I know that you care about _____ and, therefore, want him to succeed. Are you willing to make a demand to him/her that the profanity stop?" or "I have told _____ not to chew gum in class ever again. He continues to bring it in. Parents have more power to stop behaviors than teachers do. Would you be willing to demand that _____ no longer bring gum to class? Would you tell him that now?"

(d) Parent makes demand in the conference.

Teacher monitors the demand to make sure that it is not stated as a punishment, contract, or threat. If parent threatens, teacher must point out that parent is giving a choice, and that you would prefer a clear demand to stop the behavior.

(e) Referral to school counselor or administrator:

If the teacher meets with great resistance from the parents (*e.g.,* value conflicts or significant lack of parenting skills), refer them for a family-counseling session or to the principal for a school/parent conference.

# Chapter VI: Examples of Back-Up Techniques for Specific Problems

This chapter will provide examples of how some school personnel and parents have successfully dealt with specific school-related academic and behavioral problems.

## Improving Academic Performance

A junior-high-school boy in a Severely Emotionally Disturbed Class was not doing any schoolwork. This youngster compounded his problem of relatively limited academic skills by refusing to do his work. For some reason the teacher did not refer the boy until after he had completed a whole quarter without working. The teacher had been unsuccessful at using Behavior Modification coupled with encouragement and motivational techniques to get the student to do his work.

The counselor called the mother—a single parent—to come in for a conference. After eroding many of her excuses for allowing her son to continue to fail, the counselor convinced her that it was reasonable to take an active, firm stance. She decided to give clear, direct messages to him and to back up those messages. She felt that she could give clear directives, and felt that she could back them up effectively at home, but when it came to back-up techniques at school, she was uncertain what she could do to make them effective.

The counselor asked her, "What would be a clear message to your son that he has to do his work and that there is no way out of doing the work?"

She said, "The obvious thing would be to go to school and make sure that he does his work. But I am a single parent who must work. I can't possibly do that."

The counselor asked her if she could hire someone to do it for her, thereby convincing her son that he had no way out of doing his work. She indicated that she couldn't afford to do that. The counselor then asked her what time she could be at school. She said that she could be at school by 4:30 p.m. She was told that the school didn't close until 5:00. Her son was on an individualized program and had an assigned amount of work that had to be completed each day. In the event that her son had not completed the majority of his work by a fixed time, she was asked if she would be willing to come to school after work, tell him clearly and specifically that he was to do his work in school, on time, and then sit with him and make him do his work to ensure that he completed his assignments at school. She said that she would be willing to do so. She also indicated that when the school called, she would tell him on the phone, clearly and specifically, to get the work done.

A week-and-a-half later, at a follow-up conference, the mother said that her son was completing his work in class and on time. She had had to go to school only once. They were there until 7:30 that night (by pre-arrangement with the school and with the night janitor). That night he complained that he couldn't do the work, and that he was hungry, angry, and upset. She persevered and focused on the real issue—getting him to do his work. He finally got the message that there was no way out of it, that she meant business, and that he must do his work.

In many cases it will be necessary to involve other school staff members to ensure the success of the back-up technique. For this particular case it was necessary to involve the teacher, the secretaries in the main office, the principal, and the custodians. At the end of the day the teacher escorted the student to the main office, where he was placed in an adjacent room and told to stay there and work until his mother arrived. It was pre-arranged with the staff that the mother and her son would be staying at school until he completed his work and would check out with the night custodian when they left.

The success in this case was a product of the following:

(1) the erosion of the student's and the mother's belief that the student was incapable of doing the work;

(2) the mother's commitment to accept no excuses for incomplete work;

(3) the mother's clear, direct communication patterns instead of her former vague, indirect patterns;

(4) the teacher's use of clear directions instead of Behavior Modification and motivational techniques; and

(5) the development and use of a back-up technique, with the co-operation of the school staff, that conveyed to the student that there was no way out and that he must do the goal behavior.

In another case a very bright high-school junior was failing and was on the verge of being transferred to the continuation high school. The student had an I.Q. of over 132, could read and write well above grade level, and had previously gotten straight A's. After working with the psychologist, the recently remarried mother and step-father decided that the problem was serious enough that they would take over, accept no more excuses for the boy's failure, and make the boy do his work even though he did not want to do it.

The parents asked the boy what homework he had. He gave them the classic high-school response: "The teachers don't give us any homework." The parents said merely, "Anyone who gets D's and F's has homework every single night. When we get a report card from the school which indicates that you have straight B's, and the teachers say that you have no homework, then you won't have homework every single night. So where are your books?"

He replied that they were in school.

His mother said, "Okay; let's go get them." They drove to school, where they had to find a night custodian to let them in. They got his books from his locker and returned home. The parents then asked him what chapter the class was working on.

The son replied, "I don't know. The teacher is so screwed up, she's always jumping around from one place to another."

The parents responded, "You got an F the first quarter, which means that you didn't learn anything then, so we will start right from the beginning and do the work starting with Chapter One."

The boy then said, "We are working on Chapter Eight." (Isn't it amazing how memory works?) The parents told the boy to read the chapter, outline it, and answer the review questions. He told them that he was too far behind and would never be able to catch up.

The parents, using the broken-record technique, said, "We know that's the way you feel, but the only way you'll ever catch up is to start doing something right now. So start doing your work."

The boy then confronted the step-father and said, "You're not my father. You can't tell me what to do. This is the United States of America; it's not Germany, and you're not starting a Gestapo camp around here."

At this point most people would try to reason with the boy by saying, "I'm only doing this for your own good. I like you, and if you get to know me, you'll see that I'm a good guy and that I'm not trying to run your life."

Instead of falling into that trap, however, the step-father used the broken-record technique by saying, "I know that is the way you feel, *but that is not the point.* The only thing that we are talking about right now is getting you to do your homework. So start doing it right now."

Then the boy pleaded with his mother: "How could you have married this creep and let him do this to me? We had a good thing going."

The mother said, "I know that is the way you feel, but *that is not the point.* The only thing that we are talking about right now is getting you to do your homework. So start doing it right now."

There were intense emotional scenes and even some crying, but the parents were not manipulated away from the target goal. They required that the boy do his work, and demonstrated that there was no way out. They were up until 3:30 a.m. getting the boy to complete that one asssignment.

When they woke him up the next morning, he said, "You kept me up all night and put me through that emotional hell. My resistance is going to go down; I'm going to get sick, and it's all your fault."

The step-father said, "I know that's the way you feel, but let me help you get out of bed."

The boy came home from school that day without his books and homework. At this point many of us would have told the boy that he was on restriction for the next six months. Such punishment techniques would have told the boy that it was okay not to do his schoolwork as long as he was willing to take the punishment.

Instead, the parents said, "We love you very much. We are not going to punish you or belittle you, and we will not allow you to fail. You are going to be successful; there is no way out of this. Let's go get your books."

They drove to school, got the books, came home, and were up until 1:30 a.m. completing the assignment. The third day the boy brought his books home with him and completed the assignment in one hour. By the end of the semester he had earned straight B's. These parents succeeded because they were willing to do whatever was necessary to ensure that the boy was successful. The boy was convinced that his parents would have continued the program all year if needed—as, indeed, they would have done if it had been necessary.

Many teachers are extremely successful at getting students to do quality work. One dynamic, competent teacher holds a parents meeting each year during the first week of school. He tells the parents what he expects from his students and that they are not to listen to the student's complaints for the first two or three weeks. He tells the parents what he needs from them and what they are to do to make sure that the students do their homework neatly and correctly. He also guarantees that by the end of the first month the students will be doing well and liking his class. For the next few weeks the students in his class learn that they are to do all the assignments neatly and correctly and that there is no way out. He absolutely refuses to accept sloppy, incomplete, or inaccurate work. He makes them do the work over until it reaches his standards. He doesn't allow them to throw away any work. He keeps a folder for every student which contains all of their work. The first three or four weeks of school demand almost all of this teacher's time and effort. He is at school from early morning until late at night, making sure that everything is corrected and that every student knows exactly what he needs to do. The teacher is demanding and intense during this time. He makes sure that the students are on task and working. If necessary, he keeps them after school or makes them come in before school if they are behind in their work. He notifies parents every day if the student has not completed his work satisfactorily. He expects the parents to allow the student to come to school early or to stay late in order to make sure that the student is doing his work.

It is amazing to see the academic transformation of these students. As soon as they learn that the teacher means business, the quality of their work increases dramatically. The number of attempts needed to complete the work decreases drastically. When the students and the parents look through the folder of the student's work at the end of the year, they are shocked at the difference in the quality of the work between the beginning of the year and the end of the year. Both parents and students are proud of the accomplishments and of the quality of the work which the students have done.

Another example of academic success is a story from a special-education teacher about a rather "dogmatic, demanding high-school history teacher" who required his mainstreamed learning-disabled students to do the same work and tests as his other, "regular" students. He was an excellent teacher, and the only history teacher in this small rural school. He and the special-education teacher worked with these students to make sure that they did the work and learned what was necessary to be successful. The special-education teacher—because of the nature of her students' abilities and the demanding style of this history teacher—said that initially she had her doubts about their collaborative efforts. This program demanded a great deal of time from both teachers. She had to monitor these students closely. Each one of these special students passed the history course with C's or better, and every single one of them was extremely proud because he had passed a tough, regular-education course.

### Truancy from School

There are many examples of parents having to take a very active stance to stop their children from leaving school. When parents make a commitment to ensure their child's attendance, they must give clear messages to the student to go to school and to stay in school. They cannot accept any further excuses. Many parents have had to escort their student to school or hire an escort to make sure that the student got to class on time and stayed there.

"School phobia" is currently a popular psychological excuse for missing school. One boy had missed the entire first quarter of junior-high school. In reviewing his elementary-school records, the counselor found that he had a long history of absenteeism. If he came to school at all, he typically arrived, got sick, threw up, and was sent home by the school nurse. The boy had extensive medical examinations to determine the cause of his "illness". The doctors indicated that it was psychological and referred the family for private counseling. After a year of on-again, off-again individual counseling, the boy was still "school-phobic". The mother finally came to the school counselor, extremely upset. She didn't know what to do with the boy and wanted help to solve the school and home problems because his behavior was starting to jeopardize her second marriage.

The counselor persuaded her to take an active stance, to accept no further excuses for his behavior, and to make him come to school. The next day the mother escorted the boy to school and told him that he was staying, no matter what. She indicated to the school staff—and especially to the nurse—that if he threw up, he was to clean it up himself, stay in school, and do his work—no matter what. The boy never threw up in school or missed another day of school that year.

The problem with a lot of truancy cases is that many parents actively encourage the behavior. They feel that school is not very important and that it is okay for their children to miss a certain number of days. In many cases the parents actually write the excused-absence notes for their students.

One of the more interesting truancy cases involved a high-school girl who was failing and who attended school infrequently. At the family counseling session, the mother indicated that school was not especially important. She said that all of her girls knew how to read and write and were good kids. None of her girls had graduated from high school to date. The problem, as the mother saw it, was that the school continually called her about her kids' attendance. When asked about her own school days, she indicated with pride that she had not graduated from high school until she was 40 years old. Because of the mother's previous statements, the counselor was able to point out that she was a very successful mother who got her kids to do exactly what she wanted them to do. The only problem was that the school operated under the assumption that her daughters were going to graduate sometime around the age of 18, and she was operating under the assumption that they would graduate sometime around the age of 40.

She laughed and said, "You're right. I feel that you're young only once, and kids should have fun now. Later on you have to get serious and work the rest of your life."

The counselor asked her bluntly, "Since you're so successful at getting your daughter to do what you want her to do, and it is no problem to you that your daughter does not go to school or graduate—at least until she is 40—how do you plan to deal with the school? You know that they will continue to bother you about her attendance."

She sat back, thought about it for a minute, and said, "We have relatives in another state, where students have to go to school only until they are 16, and if need be I'll move her there."

The mother thanked the counselor for his honesty and bluntness, and appreciated the fact that she could see herself as a successful parent. She saw that the real problem was between her and the school and not between her and her daughter. She indicated that she could handle the school. The counselor explored with her all the possible ramifications that her actions might have on the student and asked if she and her daughter were willing to take responsibility for those possible outcomes. They both indicated that they were. After the conference was over, the counselor told the principal that the girl would not be coming to school consistently and that the principal needed to do everything legally in his power to try to keep her in school.

## Absenteeism, Period Cuts, and Tardiness

Absenteeism and period cuts are a continual junior-high and high-school problem, especially in some California school districts. In an effort to keep up with the problem, some schools have computerized their attendance procedures and hired extra employees to keep the massive records necessary to monitor student attendance. Most of these schools have also developed a fair and elaborate attendance policy to keep the student informed of the number of cuts he has taken and to allow him to make his own choices, be responsible for himself, and pay the consequences of his actions. Most of these schools use a variation of the "Five-, ten-, or fifteen-period absence" policy. On the fifth absence the parents are notified, on the tenth there is a parent conference, and on the fifteenth the student is dropped from the class. If the student is dropped from two or more classes, he is dropped from the comprehensive high school and sent to the continuation high school.

In a majority of schools, within the first three months 50-70% of the students have taken their allowed four cuts—and then they never take another cut for the rest of the year in order to avoid parental notification by the school. A smaller percentage of students, who are willing to pay the consequences of parent notification, take up to nine cuts and then never take another cut for the rest of the year in order to avoid a parent conference. Another percentage of students, who are willing to pay the consequences of the parent conference, take fourteen cuts and then never miss another class for the rest of the year in order to avoid being dropped from the course. A few students, who don't like school and want either to drop out or to go to the continuation high school, take the fifteen cuts in all of their courses. By implementing this attendance policy, these schools are encouraging students to cut classes as long as they are willing to pay the consequences of their actions. This policy forces the attendance personnel to deal with a high percentage of students who cut classes. Before this policy was implemented, the attendance personnel had to deal with only the very small percentage of students who were willing to buck the system no matter what rules were in force.

Since education is supposed to be one of the nation's top priorities, it is unfortunate that society does not value it enough to make sure that children go to school and stay in school.

In an effort to stop period cuts, some schools have instituted policies to support the idea that school is important and that students need to be in class. These schools have developed procedures to make sure that students are in the classrooms and to prevent them from leaving campus. They have set up a "no cut" policy and use an escort service to make sure that students get to class. This escort service is composed of teachers, administrators, custodians, aides, or even the parents, if need be. The escort's job is to ensure that students are in class. When a student is out of class without permission, an escort accompanies him to class and tells him to stay there. The students quickly get the message. This simple technique works.

All schools are successful at getting their students to class at certain times. On days when educators consider attendance to be especially important (such as state testing days, or during Final Exams), attendance records show a tremendous decrease in period absences and truancy. If the staff explored how they were successful in reducing the period cuts on these important days, they would realize that they gave the students no choice. The staff felt that it was important that students be in class, and they backed up their demands by making sure that the students went to class.

Recently, the superintendent of Boston City Schools said that on any given day at the high-school level they have 40% absenteeism—although on those days that are extremely important to the district, the absentee rate drops to 8-10%.

Obviously, school personnel do not make a firm commitment to having the students in class on "ordinary" days of the year. If they really wished to reduce the period cuts and the massive amounts of paperwork necessary to monitor them, they could implement a "no cut" policy and develop back-up techniques to support it. Even though they had some trouble with truancy and period cuts back in "the old days", I'm sure that the percentage of the total student body involved, as well as the total percentage of cuts, was much lower than it is today.

## Going to Physical Education

At the junior-high and high-school levels a few students do not like Physical Education, and they consistently cut that class. A related problem is that a few students will not take a shower following P.E.

The interventions are simple. If the student is not going to P.E., he needs an escort. It doesn't matter who the escort is—parent, teacher, administrator, aide, or parent-hired escort. The escort goes to the class before P.E. and, when the bell rings, he meets the student and escorts him to P.E., making sure that he dresses and stays in class for the whole period. After the student has been going to class successfully for a while and has gotten the message that he will not be allowed to fail this course, the escort can back off in small increments in order to let the student take responsibility for getting himself to class.

If taking a shower after P.E. is an important issue for the school and the parents, students who refuse to shower must be compelled to do so. In one situation a junior-high-school boy refused to take a shower. The mother was divorced and had to work; and she could not come to the school to make him take a shower. At the school/parent conference, she strongly indicated that she wanted him to be in P.E. and to take a shower. The counselor asked her if it would be all right if he or another member of the school staff escorted him to the shower and made him take one. She indicated that this would be okay. For the next few days the counselor escorted the student to P.E. After class the counselor returned and along with the P.E. teacher gave the student the choice either to take off his clothes and take a shower on his own, or they would take off his clothes for him and make him take a shower. He chose to take a shower on his own. After one or two sessions the counselor started to systematically back off and let the student take responsibility for himself. He went to P.E. and took a shower for the rest of the semester. He had gotten the message.

The mother initially believed that the boy was too shy to take a shower because he was going through secondary sex changes. She was afraid that the other boys would make fun of him. At the two-week follow-up conference the boy was asked how things were going in P.E.

He said, "Fine."

He was asked if he was playing with the other kids and having fun.

He said, "Yes."

He was asked if anyone was teasing him or causing any trouble about taking a shower.

He said, "No."

The counselor asked him if there was anything that was a problem or anything that the counselor could do to help.

The boy said, "No; everything's fine, and I can handle it."

The mother was asked if there were any problems or concerns. She said, "No; things are going well."

The P.E. teacher also indicated that things were going well and that there were no problems. The mother reported that the boy had indicated to her that he liked the class, and besides making the positive changes at school, he had been much more pleasant around the house lately.

## Littering and Lunch-Related Problems

On some high-school and junior-high-school campuses, after the nutrition break and lunch period the litter is so bad that the schools have implemented a "hose down" policy after "the animals" have left. The custodians spend most of their time cleaning up the litter, instead of doing the school maintenance jobs for which they were hired. Many school policies and attempts to solve this problem are variations of the "If/Then Contract". Here, other school activities are made contingent upon a certain number of clean days. (For example, if there are ten clean campus days, the students may have a school dance.) These contingencies miss the point; further, they inadvertently reinforce an unfortunate mode of conduct: Don't do anything unless there is something in it for you. Instead of dealing directly with the problem, school personnel let the students decide whether or not the campus will be clean (only if the students really want to go to the dance). Notice also that a few students who cannot stand anything as "square" as a school dance will now hold sort of a veto power over the other students who pick up their trash and would enjoy a dance. In instituting such a policy, the school personnel trap themselves into a never-ending escalation of reward to "motivate" the students to keep the campus clean.

This motivational technique does not always work, though, for a number of reasons: (1) some students do not want to clean up after themselves and are not motivated to do so by bribes or rewards; (2) some have learned that they don't really have to clean the place up because the school will pay somebody else to do it; and (3) some students simply enjoy the challenge of beating the system. Thus the majority of the students on campus will pay for the behavior of these few. In a sense, the kids who act appropriately are held hostage by those who don't care.

If school personnel really want to have a clean campus, then they cannot leave it up to the students to decide whether or not the campus will be clean. They must inform students that there will be no littering and that the campus will be kept clean. For a period of time they must make a concerted effort to stop the littering until the students get the message that this is a rule which is going to be enforced. School personnel will know that the students have received the message when the campus is clean.

Teachers must tell all the students clearly and specifically that from now on there is no more littering on campus. All school personnel (teachers, aides, janitors, and so forth) must be instructed that anytime they see any littering on campus they are to tell the students to pick up the trash, put it into the trash can, and never litter again. Personnel should not allow themselves to be manipulated by students ("I didn't put it there—it's not my trash", for example). They can simply use the broken-record technique and make them pick up the trash: "Regardless of whether or not this is your trash, pick it up and put it in the trash can." Initially, it may be necessary to institute a closely monitored five-to-ten-minute clean-up period (on the students' time) prior to returning to class after break and lunch. If the clean-up period extends into class time, then students must stay later in the day to make up the time that was lost. Parents of repeat litterers must come onto campus to give their child a clear message never to do that again. If need be, for a period of time, they can escort their student during break and lunch to ensure that he doesn't litter.

At one elementary school the students must raise their hands when they are finished eating. Then, on getting permission from the noon aide, they take their trash to the garbage can, pick up a sponge, walk back and clean the area where they were seated, and return the sponge before they are excused to play outside. Yet in the same school district another school "can't" control the students during lunch and the cafeteria looks like a garbage pit.

Students who learn to pick up after themselves are more likely to become environmentally responsible adults. After some professional sporting events the clean-up costs are more than $20,000. Ask any movie-theater manager about clean-up costs after the customers leave. Look at the litter on the streets, beaches, parks, and recreation areas. It is obvious that many of today's adults apparently never learned when they were children to pick up after themselves, or they have learned the lesson but don't care either because everyone lets them get away with ignoring it or because they rationalize that they "paid" for the service, making it appropriate for someone else to clean up. Sometimes students mirror parental standards, thoughts, and feelings. You may have heard a student say something like this: "It's okay. It's no big deal. That's what they pay the custodians for anyway."

### Gangs, Fights, and Inappropriate Language

It is not safe to walk on many campuses these days. Extortion, fist-fights, beatings, and rapes occur with alarming frequency, and are often the result of gang activity. Some inner-city schools resemble prisons, with tall fences surrounding the school and with security men guarding the entrance gates and escorting female faculty members. The language heard is often offensive, and the general atmosphere is not conducive to learning or to a sense of well-being. Of course, the problems and issues are complex. One approach will not solve all the problems involved, and any interventions should be part of a total community program that accentuates and encourages pride and self-respect. However, at some point a firm, active stance has to be taken to stop these extreme inappropriate behaviors.

Several positive steps can be taken to alleviate these campus-wide problems. Prior to the opening of the school year, the administration should mandate parent/student back-to-school nights in which the policies, rules, and regulations of the campus are spelled out, clearly and specifically. At these meetings, parental belief-systems and communication patterns would be discusssed along with appropriate back-up techniques. Parents would also be required to sign a form-letter stating that they agree with the rules and regulations and are willing to actively support them by giving clear messages to their child to act appropriately and to help teachers to back up the rules.

Another step would be to identify students with a history of severe and inappropriate behavior. On the very first violation teachers must demand that their parents escort these students to and from each class and sit with them in class to control them. This procedure should be carried out until the student demonstrates that he can act appropriately on his own. One school in which this procedure was carried out reported that having the parents on campus not only stopped the inappropriate behavior of that particular student but that of many other students as well. Within two days the atmosphere of the school had changed. The fights, truancies, and inappropriate behavior had dropped off drastically. Learning also improved because with parents present in the classroom the students did more work and teachers were better prepared.

Interventions such as these work when the administration clearly states and willingly enforces a policy of no inappropriate behavior in the school. However, some district-level policies and procedures are amazingly inconsistent. One rather large city school district insisted that all summer-school students and their parents sign a form stating that there would be no discipline problems in the school. The district refused to put up with any discipline problems, expected the students to be responsible and to obey the school rules, expected teachers to teach and not to put up with any inappropriate behavior, and expected the parents to actively support this policy. The administrators reasoned that since the majority of the summer-school students were there by their own choice, it would be reasonable not to accept *any* inappropriate behavior. As a result, there were few, if any, discipline problems in the summer school.

However, these same administrators reasoned that since *not* all the students were in school of their own choice during the regular school year, it was unreasonable to take the same assertive stance regarding inappropriate behavior. Accordingly, they had a lot of inappropriate, hostile, and destructive behavior from their "uncontrollable" students.

## Parents Who Will Not Come To School
## To Help Solve Discipline Problems

A school with a high proportion of children of low-income factory- and migrant-workers had difficulty in getting some of the parents to come to school to help solve the discipline problems with their children. Since many of these parents did not have telephones and did not respond to letters which were sent home, the school decided to take drastic measures. With support from the superintendent and the principal, the school counselor devised a plan to force the parents to help solve the discipline problems. Anytime a student acted inappropriately and the parents could not be notified or they did not respond to the school's letters, the counselor drove the student to the parent's place of work and told the parent that the student was not acting appropriately in school and that he was suspended to the parent's supervision for the rest of the day; that it was the parent's responsibility to tell the student to act appropriately in school and to help back it up; that anytime the student acted inappropriately, he would be suspended and delivered to the parent's place of work for supervision. The parents were informed that state law mandated that when a student was suspended, he had to be under parental supervison. Furthermore, they were told that the youth-diversion officer from the police department would make unscheduled visits, and if the parents were not supervising their child, they would be cited and taken to court. In addition, they were told that the school expected to see the student back in school the next day with his classwork and homework for the day done neatly and correctly.

The school and district-level administratiors received newspaper coverage and complaints from the community for the first few weeks of this program. However, they believed that the issue was important, so they maintained their position. The message that education is important and that the school would not put up with any inappropriate behavior was clearly communicated—not only to the parents, but also to the students. When the parents realized that the school meant business and was not going to back down, and when they felt pressure from their employers to get the problem solved, drastic changes took place. By the end of the month, the school-level personnel said that the whole atmosphere of the school had turned around. Absenteeism and discipline problems were greatly reduced. Morale of the teachers was high. They saw positive results in academic as well as behavioral areas. They also felt that they were being supported by the administration for the first time in a long time. Because of the administrators' stand, the teachers were more willing to take an active, firm stance to prevent any further inappropriate behavior in their classrooms. This policy, then, led to further improvement in the school educational environment.

## Specialty Areas in Which Schools Have Been Successful

In one high school, the principal decided to improve the total school's reading scores. He required half-an-hour of quiet reading time each day, not only from the students but also from the entire staff. He instituted reading programs and incentives to improve the level of reading as well as to encourage the joy of reading. During reading time, everyone was in class, was quiet, and was reading. There was no way out. Everyone had to do it, and the program was successful. Remarkably, at other periods of the day teachers had difficulty in keeping the students in class and working on task.

Safety and parking concerns lead some schools to require that parents picking up students park their cars in a straight line, in marked parking zones. The students go to their parent's car and stand in a painted square by the car until all students are in place. On a whistle command, all the students get into their cars. Finally, when all the students are in the cars, the cars move out in order. Then, and only then, is another set of cars allowed on campus to pick up other students in the same manner.

Schools that have institutionalized programs like Assertive Discipline are usually very successful. However, on closer examination one finds that they are successful on the third, fourth, or fifth attempt, depending on the number of checks on the board, the choices given, and the consequences. This is like the parents who tell their child to do something, and then count to Three or some other magical number. Just before the parents say the magical number, the child does the requested behavior. The parents are capable of being equally successful on the first attempt if they changed their magical number to One. Assertive Discipline, even though successful in its own right, could get the students to behave on the first infraction instead of waiting until the fifth check on the board.

# Chapter VII: Teachers' Concerns

In a question-and-answer format this chapter will focus on, and attempt to alleviate, the concerns which teachers often express about using this method in their classrooms.

*Question:* I don't want to have to tell my students what to do and how to do it all the time. I want them to grow up, be independent, and make their own decisions. By using this method, won't I condition the student to be dependent?

*Response:* No. First, this is not a child-rearing technique, nor is it a total classroom-management technique, and you are not telling your students what to do and how to do it in all areas of their lives. You are using this technique only in dangerous or non-negotiable situations. But even in these non-negotiable areas you are not really fostering dependency. When you analyze it, your operational definition of independent, responsible, mature behavior is having your students do what you think is appropriate. When they demonstrate good judgment, you let them make their own decision, and you say that they are independent and mature. Every major socialization task (toilet-training, eating with utensils, learning to read, and so forth) was initiated by others. Initially, the child may not have wanted to do these tasks, but after he learns them well no one needs to prompt him any more. He does them on his own. Because the student is doing what is expected of him, we say that he is mature and independent. In the same manner, once the student starts doing what you want him to do in a specific problem-area, establishes a pattern of being successful in this area, and internalizes the process—you will see him as being more independent, mature, and capable. Also, after he establishes the habit-pattern and knows that you mean what you say, you will *not* have to "always be telling him". Initially, structure tasks for success so that he will internalize the behavior and will eventually do in his own way what is to be done. Then you won't have to put up with the inappropriate behavior for the rest of the school year, and he won't have to suffer the consequences of his behavior for the rest of his life. When children are initially being toilet-trained, for example, they are given more structure and guidance and are told to go to the bathroom more often. As they demonstrate their ability to be successful to know when to head for the bathroom, they are usually seen as being more mature and independent. How many 16-year-olds are still dependent upon their mothers to tell them when to go to the bathroom? Life-long dependency is not created by giving clear messages and having children master designated skills. In the same fashion, students who have been given structure and guidance and thereby acquire adequate academic skills and read well are generally considered to be more "mature" and can work more independently than can students who do not have the skills and cannot read.

*Question:* I know that I can make him do it. But I would like him to want to do it on his own. Is there a way to make him like it?

*Response:* No. You cannot make anyone want, like, or love to do anything. You can't make someone whistle while he works. You can make him do the specific behavior (namely, work), but you can't control his subjective reactions (being happy enough about his work to want to whistle). The best that you can hope for is that after doing the behavior for a period of time in a supportive, reinforcing environment, the person will find it rewarding enough that he chooses to continue doing the behavior. But liking the behavior is not the issue. Some people hated school but never ditched a class. There are brothers and sister who do not love one another, yet would not physically hit each other. Conversely, there are parents who say how much they love their children, yet physically abuse them regularly. Is the behavior important enough to you to make him do it, whether or not he wants to or likes to? If so, then make him do it. If you set up the most supportive, encouraging, positive environment possible, he will probably come to like doing the behavior. Do everything in your power to set the stage to make him like it, but if that strategy does not work and the behavior is important, then make him do it, and just hope that someday he will like it and choose to do it on his own.

When learning any new major socialization task, most people do not initially like it or think that it is fun. As they gain some skill at the task, develop a habit of doing it, and get some type of reinforcement or reward for it, the majority gain some sense of pride, accomplishment, and mastery. Some of them even learn to like the task, eventually. Ask any bright, successful high-school student if he has an inborn love of history, calculus, Latin, or geometry. You will see that some folks just do what is necessary, act appropriately, and are successful, without neccessarily liking everything that they do. Maybe if someone does some particular task or skill well, he will get some form of intrinsic or extrinsic reinforcement and will eventually like it, but there is no absolute guarantee that that will happen. The only thing that you can count on is that you will probably increase the odds of someone's liking it if they can do it well. This contention that you must like something before you will do it is similar to the parental belief that you have to love your sister before you can stop fighting with her or hitting her. You cannot control love, but you can control hitting or verbally teasing and abusing your sister. Stop the brother/sister knock-down, drag-out fights and verbal abuse, and you will increase the chances of the brother and sister growing to like each other and possibly even to love each other. In the same vein, if you get Johnny to read well, he will probably like reading better than does Mary, who still has to struggle with each word on the page. As a general truism of life: If a student has mastered a task and does it very well, the chances are good that he *might* like to do it. But if he has not mastered the task or is embarrassed by the fact that he can't do it well, the chances that he will like it are *greatly* reduced.

*Question:* What about self-concept and self-esteem? Don't you need to get the student to feel better about himself before you can implement all of these changes?

*Response:* No. Get the student to change and to act appropriately, and he will feel better about himself. A good majority of what we typically call self-concept or self-esteem is related to what we can do and what we actually do. Therefore, if a student has a low self-concept, is not able to read, and is failing, then he *needs* to read and to pass his courses in order to help to improve his self-concept.

Granted, good grades do not guarantee a good self-concept, but at least if a student can read well and gets good grades, then he will have fewer impediments to developing and maintaining a good self-concept. Even though good grades do not necessarily equal good self-concept, poor reading skills and poor grades in this country do generally lead to a poorer self-concept.

*Question:* What about demanding too much? Doesn't it put too much stress on students? What about the high expectations and demands of the Japanese and their high rate of suicide among students?

*Response:* It's not the expectations or the clear demands that provoke suicide. Rather, it is the context in which these expectations are made. If the expectations are communicated in a hostile, non-caring, guilt-inducing, shame- and/or fear-producing way, then the student will feel that he is "no good" unless he lives up to these standards. Within this emotional context the student will run a high risk for a wide range of maladaptive behaviors, including suicide. However, if realistic expectations are communicated in a context of positive encouragement, love, respect, and joy of learning for its own sake, then the student usually becomes an individual who is highly skilled and competent in a wide range of endeavors.

*Question:* Should you use this method with very young children or students, and, if so, does it work?

*Response:* Again, this is not a child-rearing technique, nor a total classroom-management program, and it should not be used in all situations. You don't need to bring out the cannons to get the child to eat peas. Use the lowest level of disciplining that is necessary to get the job done. This method is most appropriately used for behaviors which are "non-negotiable" and that have been demonstrated to be within the student's level of capability. Make a distinction between learning a new skill and performing a known skill. Most very young children are learning new skills rapidly. At this stage, you need to spend more time with them to help them to learn effective habit-patterns, so that they acquire the skills necessary to be successful. During this period of rapid acquisition of skills, you need to use good parenting and teaching techniques to ensure success. For instance, you would not think of demanding that a two-year-old be completely toilet-trained on his first attempt. Rather, you would encourage the youngster; you would set up positive expectancies; you would watch and control the environment and the child a little more; and you would give yourself and the child more time to be successful. However, if you have a twelve-year-old who started soiling his pants, you could reasonably demand that he stop that behavior immediately.

Most children understand demands for appropriate behavior at a fairly young age and are capable of doing what is requested. They are certainly capable of learning what behaviors are unacceptable and non-negotiable: sticking anything into the electrical sockets, playing in the street, playing with Dad's expensive stereo equipment, and other unacceptable behaviors.

Love your children and your students, be patient with them, take the time to teach them what you want, but also have realistically high expectations for them and demand appropriate behavior from them if they are not willing to do it on their own.

*Question:* It seems that in some cases this more straightforward, assertive approach might actually cause more problems and escalate the situation to a real confrontation of wills. Is there a better way of dealing with students, without having to confront them on everything?

*Response:* First, don't confront students on everything. Confront them only in the areas that are non-negotiable "must" behaviors, and only after you have tried your other favorite methods. Again, if you can use any other approach and it works, use it. For example, low-keyed genuine caring humor works well in most situations.

If you are having a serious problem with a student, however, it is probably because he has a long history of inappropriate behavior, and you have already tried your favorite methods. At this point try the straightforward approach.

When I look back on my own teaching career, I never really had any serious discipline problems in my classroom. I was friendly and easy-going and used humor and a lot of humanistic psychology to motivate my students. I had good skills at de-escalating tense situations, and I rarely had to confront students. Because of my non-confrontational style, I ended up with a lot of the marginal students. These students never caused any trouble, but they never did much work, either. I now wonder what would have happened if I had been just as humanistic but challenged them and made them do the work. They would have been considerably better off in the long run, I now suspect.

I see nice kids who can't read or write well go through junior-high school, high school, and college. I think about the disservice which we are doing to these young people when we pass them along without confronting them and making them do the work. Yes, I'm sure that if you abandon your "cool" attitude and challenge students, you might see escalated manipulative behavior. But, as professional educators, we must see beyond these manipulations to the painful, self-defeating traps in which these students are caught. We have to help them, guide them, encourage them, and if need be make them do the work. If education is important, then we must make it happen. Helen Keller did not initially want to learn to read, to write, or to behave. When confronted directly, she at first increased her resistance. Sometimes in education there *will* be a confrontation of wills. The real issue is this: Is it important enough to make the student do the requested behavior, even if the student doesn't want to do it and he therefore escalates the issue? Are you willing to do whatever it takes to make it happen, and can you do it with love and caring in your heart, with an objective view that sees the value of the end result? Can you do it without hurting yourself or the student— without breaking the student's spirit, freedom, or will?

If you still question the value of having some non-negotiable behaviors, please read in the Appendix the account of Helen Keller and her great teacher, Anne Sullivan Macy; it is a famous example of perseverance which examines this very question that we have been discussing: Is the end result worth the aggravation of the initial confrontation?

*Question:* This method depends a lot upon parental support. What happens if you don't get their support? What happens when you work with parents who really don't care?

*Response:* You'd be surprised at how much you can do as a teacher to get students to behave without parental support. Marva Collins, who started her own school in Chicago, helps to prove this contention. She taught low-income students and did not have a lot of parental support, to say the least. She expected her students to learn and to behave, and she went to great lengths to ensure that they did both. Besides, most parents really do care about their kids and want the best education for them. Although some parents are not so sophisticated nor so well-educated as we might like, that fact does not mean that they don't care or that they are not willing to help. Parents are our best allies. We need to develop ways to let parents know that we want to work with them as a team, that we respect their position, and that we are not going to make them feel inadequate. Some teachers operate under the myth that parents don't want to help and are the enemy. Granted, some parents are not very supportive, but the majority are, and we need to develop more effective ways of working with them.

To the very small percentage of parents who are not supportive, the district needs to state clearly the school's position: Education is important, and students must act appropriately. The counselor who drove the students to their parents' places of work clearly exemplifies this commitment to making education happen. Last-ditch school-based efforts designed to force the parents to make a clear stand, either for or against education and appropriate behavior, should be planned—and integrated, if need be, with pressures and back-up techniques from community, legal, mental-health, and child-protective agencies.

*Question:* Do you believe in suspending students?

*Response:* Suspension is an "If/Then" contract—"If you do that again, then you will be suspended." The problem with suspension is that some students don't like school, and they don't want to be in school, anyway. Ask yourself what you want the student to do: Would you rather have him in school developing the skills necessary to be successful, or do you want him missing school, missing his assignments, and getting farther behind? If you want him in school acting appropriately and doing his work, then develop interventions designed to keep him in school. Put all your time and energy into making the student do the work; don't send him home or out onto the streets. Sometimes educators fall into the trap of doing what the student really wants to do in the first place.

All of this reminds me of the story of a woman who had a prize-winning rose garden. A groundhog got into her garden and started to eat all the roots of her champion roses. In an all-out effort to control this hungry rodent, the woman tried everything—poisons, pouring water down the holes, and so on. Finally, in desperation, she started to dig up the whole garden. The groundhog, when finally trapped, made a break for freedom. The woman, chasing after it, finally hit it with her shovel and had it pinned down. She said to it, "I should kill you right away, but that would be too good for you. You've made me suffer. I need to make you suffer for all the hurt that you have caused me." After thinking it over, she finally came up with an idea that would really make him pay the price for all of his misdeeds: she buried him alive.

In a high-school counseling group, at the end of the session a student lit a cigarette. The counselor told him to put out the cigarette. He said, "No, I won't." The counselor walked over to him and told him again to put out the cigarette. The student said that if the counselor wanted it out, he would have to put it out himself. Seeing this as a "confrontation of wills", the counselor wrestled the cigarette away from him and put it out. Defiantly, the student said, "So what are you going to do about it? Are you going to suspend me? Go ahead; I dare you. I don't care if I'm suspended."

The counselor told him, "No, I am not going to suspend you. I like you, and you need to be in my class learning about human nature and yourself. It is very important for you to be here. The only issue that we are talking about now is smoking. So no more smoking ever again in this class." Just then the school bell rang, and the counselor pointedly addressed the student, "See you tomorrow." The student nodded and left the counseling room, taking a short-cut through the front office. When confronted by a secretary, he sassed her and left the building. The principal, who had overheard his comment, came out of his office and went after the student. When confronted, the student made another impudent comment. The principal responded by saying, "If you keep this up, you are suspended." The student replied, "Big f_____ deal!" The principal's reaction was, "You just earned yourself a vacation—you're suspended."

Sometimes we do just what the student wants us to do, and—just like the woman in her rose garden—we "bury the groundhogs alive".

While suspension works with some students, especially if the student is compliant or motivated, it does not work with difficult students who don't really want to be in school anyway. The only times when suspension would be useful is either when you have no effective pre-plannned, individual lesson-plan back-up technique and you need to get the student out of your class temporarily, or as a strategy to force the parents to meet with school personnel to resolve the differences between home and school. In the first of these two situations, this would be an in-school suspension until you could get the parents to come in for a conference. In the second situation, the suspension is not intended as an "If/Then" contract for the student. It would be intended, instead, to put pressure on the parents to come in and to take an active stance to support the school's efforts to educate their child. Some school personnel in the state of Connecticut recently related that one student had fifty days of accumulated suspensions from school because he was truant from school! Is this school district's policy of suspensions working? Is it meeting the educational needs of the student?

*Question:* This method gives more power to teachers and parents. Some of them will misuse it. Don't you think that you need some safeguards against the misuse of power?

*Response:* Parents and teachers already have the power. The problem is that too many teachers and parents who are having difficulty with students are already misusing *their* power and are reacting by punishing students daily. The issue is not whether parents or teachers have the power. The real issue is whether they use the power which they already have in a healthy, productive way or whether they use it in a hostile, negative, punitive way. When used properly, this particular discipline approach safeguards students against verbal and physical abuse, and decreases the need for punishment.

Of course, in the real world some teachers and some parents do misuse their power. Parents who misuse their power should be referred to your school counselor, school psychologist, or private clinician to help them to clarify those problems and to develop skills necessary to achieve their desired family goals within the context of a healthier environment. Teachers who misuse their power may need further skill-training in this method, or they may need some guidance and close supervision from the site administration to ensure a more positive educational environment.

If a teacher is misusing her position and power, then the administrator must supervise the teacher and make clear the district's expectations, goals, and demands. One of the problems in education, as well as in many businesses, is that a lot of administrators or supervisors do not give clear directions and expectations to their employees. If, however, they are giving clear, specific, concrete messages and that process does not seem to work and the teacher continues to be a negative influence, then the administrator needs to guide the teacher into a different career.

# Conclusion

Remember: This method is not a cure-all for all of an educator's problems. It is specifically designed to stop inappropriate behavior and to get students moving in the right direction. Educational institutions must then maintain and accelerate that growth and development with quality education, curriculum, and instruction. The academic atmosphere of any school is undermined when there are on-campus problems of verbal abuse, violence, extortion, gangs, and other inattentive and disruptive behaviors. Concomitantly, the mental health and morale of students, teachers, and administrators alike are negatively affected. After working under adverse conditions for years, the staff members become pessimistic and unproductive. Students drop out—and sometimes graduate—both frustrated and unskilled. It is believed that putting a stop to inappropriate behavior is a major first step in making the school a better place in which to learn and a place in which everyone in the school community would be happier.

However, to promote and nourish the intellectual, social, and emotional growth of students, you will have to use this method in a caring, encouraging educational environment. The contention of this book is that if you can stop most inappropriate behavior in the classrooms and throughout the school, you will—by that fact alone—be improving the educational environment for all of your students and will be increasing the chances that students will be better able to utilize the quality educational opportunities that you offer them, thereby maximizing their educational opportunities and, ultimately, their human potential.

# APPENDIX
## Helen Keller and Anne Sullivan Macy*

**(A Success Story of Non-belief in Handicapping Conditions as An Excuse for Inappropriate Behavior, and of Belief in the Value of Effective Back-up Techniques)**

It was a bright, clear spark from Teacher's soul that beat back the sooty flames of thwarted desire and temper in little Helen's no-world. That spark was the word "water". Compassion in the old sense does not describe the springs of Teacher's motives. Her disbelief in nature as an unfailing friend of humanity lay back of her efforts to liberate Helen—"Phantom" I prefer to call the little being governed only by animal impulses, and not often those of a docile beast. Teacher's fight against her own blindness began in her childhood, and the partial restoration of her sight while she was in school at Perkins Institution for the Blind near Boston had not ended her struggle to maintain her ascendancy over nature. That struggle lasted as long as her earth-life.

Secretly or openly she always resented what seemed to her the purposeless evils that had marred her sight and laid waste the health, sanity, and happiness of millions throughout the world. How ruthless then was her assault upon the blindness, deafness, and muteness that bound her little pupil in triple dungeon of thwarted instincts. Boldly she resolved to put herself in the place of nature and topple it from its aimless supremacy over Helen by substituting love and inventive thought for the unconscious cruelty of the child's fate.

This is a period in Teacher's life which distresses me to remember. Naturally, I wish that after the intoxicating tide of delight that swept over her when the operations made it possible for her to read with her eyes, she might have found a child responsive to her sympathetic touch. But, alas! Phantom had no sense of "natural" bonds with humanity. All the sweetness of childhood created by friendly voices and the light of smiling faces was dormant in her. She did not understand obedience or appreciate kindness. I remember her as plump, strong, reckless, and unafraid. She refused to be led,

---

*Helen Keller, *TEACHER: Anne Sullivan Macy* (New York, New York: Doubleday and Company, 1955).

and had to be carried by force upstairs when she received her first lesson. Another time her table manners required correction. Phantom was in the habit of picking food out of her own plate and the plates of others with her fingers. Annie Sullivan would not put up with such behavior, and a fight followed during which the family left the room. Phantom acted like a demon, kicking, screaming, pinching her would-be deliverer and almost throwing her out of her chair, but Annie succeeded in compelling her to eat with a spoon and keep her hands out of her plate. Then Phantom threw her napkin onto the floor, and after an hour's battle Annie made her pick it up and fold it. One morning Phantom would not sit down to learn words which meant nothing to her, and kicked over the table. When Annie put the table back in its place and insisted on continuing the lesson, Phantom's fist flew out like lightning and knocked out two of Annie's teeth.

A sorrier situation never confronted a young woman on fire with a noble purpose. Phantom's parents were likely to interfere whenever attempts were made to discipline her. For this reason Annie won their consent to get her away to a quiet place, and at their suggestion took the child to a vine-covered annex near the homestead, Ivy Green. The furniture was changed so that Phantom would not recognize it—my smell memory, too, is different—and it was agreed that the family would come to them every day, without letting Helen know of their visits. From Teacher's later testimony I know that the two were, so to speak, caged in the annex, and I marvel that Annie dared to stay alone with such a menace to her personal safety.

Already I have referred to several fights between Annie and Phantom, not because I have any coherent or detailed remembrance of them, but because they indicated the grueling nature of the work which Teacher had undertaken. In *The Story of My Life,* which I wrote with the carelessness of a happy, positive young girl, I failed to stress sufficiently the obstacles and hardships which confronted Teacher—and there are other defects in the book which my mature sense of her sacrifice will not permit to go uncorrected.

In my memory of the annex I am conscious of a Phantom lost in what seemed to her new surroundings. I perceive sudden jerks, pulls, and blows not dealt by Annie but by Phantom herself trying to escape restraining arms. How like a wild colt she was, plunging and kicking! Certainly it was a sturdy Phantom who belabored her supposed enemy. There comes back to me a scuffle round and round an object that my touch-recollections represent as a bed, and a firm gesture of Annie to make her lie down or get up and dress.

Phantom had no sense of time, and it was years before she learned of the many exhausting hours which Annie spent trying to bring her under control without breaking her spirit. Even that had been only partly accomplished when the two went home. Then Phantom grew angry over Annie's repeated attempts to impress upon her the difference between "water" and "mug".

Tactually I recall quick footsteps in the room, a hand—my mother's—seizing Phantom and dragging her away for a sound spanking. After that, Phantom began to improve, but she still lacked the normal child's love of praise. She was not aware that she had been punished because she did not distinguish between right and wrong. Her body was growing, but her mind was chained in darkness as the spirit of fire is chained within the flint. But at last, April 5, 1880, almost exactly a month after her arrival in Tuscombia, Annie reached Phantom's consciousness with the word "water". This happened at the well-house. Phantom had a mug in her hand, and while she held it under the spout Annie pumped water into it; and as it gushed over the hand that held the mug she kept spelling w-a-t-e-r into the other hand. Suddenly Phantom understood the meaning of the word, and her mind began to flutter tiny wings of flame. Caught up in the first joy that she had felt since her illness, she reached out eagerly to Annie's ever-ready hand, begging for new words to identify whatever objects she touched. Spark after spark of meaning flew through her mind until her heart was warmed and affection was born. From the well-house there walked two enraptured beings calling each other "Helen" and "Teacher". Surely such moments of delight contain fuller life than an eternity of darkness.